My Calvary Road

By the same author . . .

THE CALVARY ROAD

WE WOULD SEE JESUS

BE FILLED—NOW

"WHEN I SAW HIM . . ."
> Where revival begins

OUR NEAREST KINSMAN
> The message of redemption and revival in the
> Book of Ruth.

FORGOTTEN FACTORS
> An aid to deeper repentance of the forgotten factors
> of sexual misbehaviour.

FROM SHADOW TO SUBSTANCE
> A rediscovery of the inner message of the Epistle to
> the Hebrews.

My
Calvary
Road

Roy
Hession

ZONDERVAN
PUBLISHING HOUSE OF THE ZONDERVAN CORPORATION
GRAND RAPIDS, MICHIGAN 49506

My Calvary Road
Copyright © 1978 by Roy Hession.

Library of Congress Cataloging in Publication Data

Hession, Roy.
　My Calvary road.

　　1.　Hession, Roy.　　2.　Evangelists—England—Biography.　　I.　Title.
BV3785.H44A35　　269'.2'0924 [B]　　78-1284
ISBN 0-310-26031-0

Printed in the United States of America

Contents

Foreword

I FIRST MET Roy in the summer of 1926 when I had been asked to lead a holiday houseparty for older schoolboys at the seaside mission at Southwold on the east coast of England. I had rarely seen such a collection of youthful enthusiasts. Every day we would think of some new escapade, and one of these was a swim around the Southwold pier. (It was twice as long as it is today.) All fifteen boys would change in our big house on the seafront and then, led by Roy, who was just eighteen and his younger brother Brian, would rush for the sea. It was Roy with his professional crawl who would lead the way swimming around the pier.

In our morning and evening prayers the Bible lit up as we saw "the Captain of the Host" appearing to Joshua, and the One who called His disciples beside the Lake of Galilee. In faith we asked God that each one of those fifteen boys would answer the call to follow Him, and to the glory of God we believe every one of them did so personally, led by Roy and Brian who never looked back. Roy seemed to take me as an elder brother, and that friendship has deepened and grown as the years have gone by.

After that time, for the next twenty years we went our various ways without seeing one another: Roy into a London bank and then into full-time evangelistic service, and I into life as a medical missionary in East Africa, coming home on leave every four years to tell of a deep movement of revival which God had graciously allowed us to experience—both the Africans and us missionaries. In 1947 a small team of us had come home with the definite vision of sharing with the Christians of England what we had been learning in revival in East Africa. A telephone call from Roy linked us up again after all those years and resulted in the team's being invited to the Bible conference houseparty which Roy was running at Matlock in the center of England. The messages, fresh from a convention in Western Uganda, were given, and afterward were written up by Roy in his book *The Calvary Road*, which also contained other chapters expressive of the new experience of Jesus that he and others in England were finding. From that time it began to go on its way around the world, reaching more than half a million copies in English alone, as well as various editions in other languages.

The same message has sent us, sometimes together, not around the pier, but around far-off parts of the world with the message of revival to North America, Brazil, India, Europe, and Africa, where the winds of the Holy Spirit have been blowing. Roy's enthusiasm is always infectious, and everywhere there are left behind those who have caught the vision.

I praise God for every memory of what He has done through Roy and his books, and I recommend those who read his own personal story to listen to the voice of the Holy Spirit calling us all to see the vision again of the glorified Lord moving "in the midst of the candlestick," and to be given again our "first love" to go all out for revival.

JOE CHURCH, M.A., M.R.C.S.

Little Shelford,
Cambridge

Preface

THIS BOOK OWES its appearance to the vision and invitation of Edward England, director of the Religious Department of Hodder and Stoughton.

In 1950 I published a little book of just sixty-three pages, *The Calvary Road,* as a result of God's meeting my own heart in revival. In the years since then it has circulated among Christians in the English-speaking world to an extent that has both astonished and humbled me, until now it has sold well over half a million copies, with its circulation not falling off with the passage of years, but rather increasing. In addition it has been translated into some forty different languages. Everywhere it has gone God has been pleased to use it to the revival of the spiritual life of needy Christians and sometimes of whole groups of them together. I have heard the most extraordinary stories of lives transformed, homes restored, and churches revived through its ministry.

One day in 1976 Edward England said to me, "You realize, don't you, that *Calvary Road* is better known than you are. People would find it helpful if they knew the personal story behind the book, and I suggest you write another entitled *My Calvary Road.*" My first reaction was negative, but on maturer reflection I came to see that such a story could be a means of making known the message and illustrating how God deals with his children. Everybody finds a first-person story absorbing, especially if he can identify it with his own life.

Then, too, I realized I had come to the time in life when it would be possible to write such a story. It would have been impossible earlier, for the pilgrimage would only have been half-traversed. But now that I am approaching seventy, and have known the Lord for fifty-two years and spent more than forty of those years itinerating with the message of Christ all over Britain and a dozen or more other countries, I can look back and see my Calvary road in perspective. In saying "see it in perspective," I mean be able to understand more fully God's dealings and rightly interpret them that others may profit by it. That is difficult except as one is able to stand back and see events in relation one to another.

So here, then, is the story of one man's pilgrimage, *My Calvary Road*. While I am thankful for all I have learned, I have to confess that nearly all of it has been through mistakes. I have come into things as a beggar at the back door rather than as a respectable visitor at the front door. By that I mean I have entered into the positive by confessing the negative and I have found that when I have done so, Jesus has brought me right into the positive blessings which I so lamentably lacked. Let those who feel themselves qualified to enter by the front door do so, if they can; I have not been able to enter but by the beggars' back door, the cross of the Lord Jesus Christ. I therefore feel it necessary to share more than a few of my mistakes and weaknesses. The reader may even identify with them and realize that he can enter that way too.

May the story, such as it is, glorify the grace of God and in His hands do something new for the reader.

Many readers will be my brothers and sisters in Christ in North America, for, whereas the original *Calvary Road* had gone right around the world, it has circulated more widely in North America than anywhere else. I have therefore felt it right to take time now and then to explain some aspects of the English scene, especially as they apply to evangelical life, so that American readers may understand better my background. I trust English readers will bear patiently when they find themselves reading explanations of things they know.

One

"Revival—The Bottom Falling Out"

IN JANUARY 1947 I placed a long-distance call to Dr. Joe Church, who had just returned to England from East Africa. During our talk he said, "The Christians of England, Roy, seem to have the strangest ideas of what revival is; they think it is the roof blowing off, when really it is the bottom falling out!"

I had not seen or spoken to Joe Church for twenty-one years. The last time had been when I was eighteen years old and had been persuaded to go to a small Christian holiday houseparty for boys in the seaside town of Southwold in Suffolk, and he had been the leader. There my long resistance to Jesus Christ ended and I let Him take over my life. Joe Church had recently qualified as a doctor and was about to go to East Africa as a medical missionary. In the intervening years I had followed his course with interest, especially when news began to arrive that God was giving His church in Rwanda and elsewhere in East Africa a deep and continuing revival, in which many were being converted, and even missionaries were making redis-coveries of Jesus Christ—and apparently Joe was in the fore-front of all this.

In 1947 he and a small team of missionaries returned to share with us in England and Switzerland what they had been learn-ing in revival. By this time the Lord had led me to leave the bank in London in which I had worked since leaving school, in order to give my time to itinerant evangelistic work on the staff of a Christian youth movement, the National Young Life Campaign. As an evangelist, I was, of course, interested in revival and dreamed that one day in one of my campaigns the Holy Spirit would work so mightily that it could be called revival. I am afraid that in my mind I would, of course, always be on the platform directing things. I did not know then that revival began with the evangelist himself. When I heard that these men had come to England, and especially as one of them had been the instrument of my own conversion to God, I invited them to be the speakers at an Easter conference I was organizing.

"Revival is not the roof blowing off, but the bottom falling out."

I chuckled as I mused over the words, and I thought it would be a good phrase to incorporate into an address! I little knew that this would be my experience in the days ahead, beginning with that very conference.

The bottom falling out: what does it mean? It is what Jesus meant when He said that the corn of wheat must fall into the ground and die if it is to bring forth fruit. It is what Daniel meant when he saw the vision of the Lord and said, "My comeliness is turned into corruption," that is, what he thought to be his righteousness he saw to be filthy rags, his fancied gains but dead losses; or, as St. Augustine put it, his virtues but splendid sins. It is what Isaiah meant when he saw the Lord and said, "Woe is me; for I am undone; because I am a man of unclean lips." The very expression, "undone," is suggestive—God undid him that day, and He did so by showing him that the most consecrated part of him, his lips (remember, Isaiah was a preacher), were unclean in God's sight, and that his very service for God was corrupted by self, initiated in self-will, carried on in self-effort, and done for self's glory. The bottom fell out for Isaiah that day; that on which he had been standing and building gave way beneath his feet. It is indeed a terrible thing for a man when his comeliness is turned to corruption.

This was what God would do for me. But it was not the work of a day. Having undone me, He was in no hurry to do me up again. He had to be sure I understood what He was teaching. There was more to be broken down than I thought, a greater reorientation than I imagined. It was a difficult time. During this period I wrote the articles that were put together in *The Calvary Road* and committed to paper the lessons of "dying to live" that others and I were learning together. But He did "do me up" again and He showed me that Christ Himself was the end of the struggle for righteousness, peace, and revival.

That for me was revival in the true sense of the word, the restoration of the first love I had left and the renewal of an experience that had grown stale. My experience in Christ had once been so fresh and I had known fruitful years as an evangelist; but something had gone wrong and I was in the midst of a sad decline, having lost the power of the Spirit— until God caused the bottom to fall out and self to be revealed for what it was. But when He "did me up" again in Christ, all that I had lost was restored and more than restored.

It is characteristic of God that when He restores, He restores more than we have lost. It is rather like us inadvertently taking a diversion from the main road. When at last we find our way back to the highway, what a joy to discover that we have returned to it further on than where we left it. It would be good to return just to the place where we departed, but to return to a place further on, that is grace indeed! I think it was Charles G. Finney who said that revival is nothing more than a series of new beginnings. True, but to that I would add, such beginnings for the penitent man are not merely in the same place, but on each occasion in a better place than where he was when he got away. This is my testimony.

Am I right to infer that my Calvary road began with this experience? It really began, as it does with all of us, when we first come to the cross of Calvary as sinners. All the elements of later and fuller experience in the Christian life are implicit in that first experience of grace, "I am a sinner, but Jesus is my Savior." Indeed, we may be suspicious of any emphasis, teaching, or experience which is not at bottom merely an extension of these simple truths. To go deeper in the Christian life is simply to realize that we are bigger sinners than we ever thought and that Jesus is a bigger Savior than we ever conceived Him to be.

That being so, the story of this man's pilgrimage must begin with his first experience of grace.

Two

The First Steps

SOME BIOGRAPHIES BEGIN by telling us that the person in question was born at a very early age! Well, I was no exception; the event took place on April 10, 1908. I was born and brought up in London suburbia in a typical middle-class English family of modest prosperity and educated as a boarder at what we are pleased to call in England a public school. I must explain that an English public school is not a public school at all as some would understand it, but a private one, much prized by those who can afford it, and in these times of inflation it takes some affording! But in those far-off days it was just within the means of my parents, and at the age of seven or so, my brother and I were packed off to boarding school. It sounds heartless, doesn't it, but we managed to survive each term until the holidays came around.

Ours was not a church-going family. My parents, uncles, aunts, and cousins were quite innocent of the gospel, though my mother, after being widowed early, nobly struggled to do the best for her two boys and to inculcate in them a healthy conscience with regard to right and wrong. She was regarded as a great beauty, and there were not lacking suitors who offered her remarriage. They would, of course, have to take on her two schoolboy sons and, I am afraid, we gave them no encouragement. We wanted our mother to ourselves! She on her part did not find it too great a hardship to refuse them, as she was very willing to put her sons' interests above her own. The only "brush" she had ever had with the gospel—and it was only a "brush"—was in her teens when Moody and Sankey were having meetings in London. An enthusiast approached her and her sisters in the street and asked, "Are you saved?"

When, however, I was sent to boarding school, I had to attend school chapel, and in due time I was confirmed along with many others. But the bishop, dear man, who laid his hands on my head only confirmed me in my sins. I knew nothing of God's good news for sinners. Yet I took my confirmation seriously and tried to turn away from the sins that come into every schoolboy's life. I remember when I took my first Communion struggling to realize God's presence and my mind reeling in the attempt. Any good effects soon wore off and I was back to where I was before. There were moments when I was conscious of God stirring in my heart, as for instance, when we sang in chapel, "At even 'ere the sun was set, . . ." but then who has not been moved by the gentle pathos of that hymn, especially if he is singing the lovely tenor part in the choir.

God took the initiative in bringing me to Himself and He did so through a cousin, training to be an officer in the Royal Navy. He was led to Christ by a fellow cadet and immediately proceeded to share his faith with the rest of the family, much to their shock. I myself received a letter from him in which he spoke enthusiastically about Jesus Christ and urged me to turn over my life to Him. I was not only shocked, but disgusted; I thought it indecent to be enthusiastic about God and Christ; my experience in school chapel had not led me to expect anything but boredom from the Deity. In any case, I wanted to run my own life and go my own way.

My cousin, however, persisted and I was offered a winter sports holiday in Switzerland with a party run by the Officers' Christian Union, which existed to draw together Christian officers in the services, and with which he was now associated. The party consisted of young officers—no women among them—many of whom had recently become Christians; others became such before my eyes. I can see now that it was the best introduction I could have had to virile, personal Christianity, but I hated it and decided I would have nothing to do with

Jesus Christ and returned home feeling very miserable. When I got back to boarding school I tried to tell the others, hoping they might feel as convicted and miserable as I did. Of course, they did not know what I was talking about and I only gained for myself the epithet of "the Salvation Army man." I was nothing of the sort, but I had been exposed to something that I could not shake off.

Finally in August 1926 just as I left school, my brother Brian and I were prevailed upon to go to a small Christian holiday camp (it was actually held in a house); it was the only holiday I was offered that year, and I knew my cousin had been behind it and my mother encouraged it. This was led, as has been mentioned, by Dr. Joe Church, shortly to go for the first time as a medical missionary to Rwanda. Although there would be fun and games, I knew the main purpose would be spiritual. The prospect of three weeks of living in that atmosphere seemed too much for me, and I dreaded it. The Lord had been pursuing me and had now got me in a corner, and I doubted if I could hold out for so long. The men running the camp were young university students, some of them good athletes, and I had to confess that Jesus Christ had not spoiled life for them. One day, as I listened to a medical student at a garden meeting, I saw the cross, God loving me and laying my sins on His Son. All my opposition was melted down, and I said to myself, "Why in the world am I so scared? That does not look like the act of One who is against me and who would make my life miserable!" A night or two later, when someone had been speaking of Christ knocking on the door of the human heart, I got away from the rest and walked up and down the sea front and prayed, "Lord Jesus, if You've never come into my heart before, come now." I had had so much exposure to the gospel in those days that I did not know whether I had actually opened the door to Him or not, but I decided that if I had not done so, I would do it there and then.

That night I experienced peace with God for the first time: "being justified by faith I had peace with God." Next day I confessed all this to others in the camp and that made everything final. "I had opened my mouth to the Lord and I could not go back"—and I did not want to. The joy of the Lord so filled my heart and intimacy with Him was so real that when I knelt to pray by my bed (a new thing for me) I did not want to rise. I had taken the first step into those "good works that God had before ordained that I should walk in them" and I little knew than how good that plan of His was going to be or where it would take me. I had been apprehended by Christ Jesus, and the initiative had been wholly His.

My brother Brian had come to faith in Christ the year before. Under the stimulus of this year's camp he went forward at a speed that left me standing. He had another year at boarding school, where he started a Christian Union. He was determined from the start to get into the ministry, and having obtained a church grant to take him to Cambridge University, he went into the Church of England. In the last years of his life (he was fifty-two when he died) he became what one may call "England's best-known invalid." He had contracted cancer, involving him in operation after operation; in his last seven years he wrote seven books, from *Determined to Live* to *Bridge to God*, in which he told how Christ enabled him to rise above the challenge of cancer to his faith, books which sufferers all over the English-speaking world found enormously helpful. His ministry was often heard on the radio, and the press loved him. The whole nation followed the course of his illness. When he died, his death was splashed over the national dailies and with it a noble testimony to Christ.

I started more slowly. Shortly after we returned from Southwold, Brian was asked to give a message at a small mission hall in London, and I accompanied him. I was impressed to hear my young brother speak with such clarity, earnestness, and power at his first attempt, but not so impressed when the organizers, appreciating what they had heard, asked his older brother if he would give them a date too. I refused the suggestion outright, but Brian, flushed with the joy of being used by the Lord, urged me strongly to do it. Very reluctantly I assented. But when that ominous date came around, I conveniently "forgot" it and never showed up. I never inquired afterward what happened at the other end—I just didn't want to know! If I should be asked how my itinerant ministry of forty years or more began, well, that is how it started—with the sermon that never was!

In the early days I had to battle with doubts. On one occasion I was in such an agony as to whether God was real and the Bible true that I had to put my pen down on the desk in the bank where I worked and go to the washroom and pace the floor.

It was not long before I was challenged as to who was going to be lord in my life—I or Christ? I had always followed crazes. The male of the species is prone to take up this hobby or that interest and pursue it with passionate exclusiveness—at least this male did. He differed from others perhaps, in that having pursued a thing intensely for a time, he would drop it and take up something else equally intensely. So much was this the case that when I became converted and transferred my interest to spiritual things, my mother thought it was just another craze, soon to be dropped. I half-wondered myself. I was so relieved when, after a year of my new life, I could say, "Praise the Lord, I'm still walking with Him; it's not one of my crazes after all!" There were, however, several legacies of those days obtruding into the new life, with which God had to deal.

Two crazes had been running concurrently. One was playing the trumpet. I had graduated from playing the bugle in the school band to a brass cornet, and from that to a silver-plated trumpet! Hour after hour I practiced, to the discomfort of everyone within earshot, and I had a few lessons from a famous trumpet player. This led me to play in an amateur symphony orchestra, and it was a great day when we had the opportunity to play once on BBC radio—I was only the fourth trumpeter, with little heard of me! There in my bedroom would lie my beautiful trumpet, eyed with such love and surrounded with so many dreams of myself as a great musician one day. The fantasies seem ludicrous now, but that trumpet had taken precedence in my affections over the Lord Jesus Christ.

The other craze was athletics. The Christian movement with which I had become associated, the Crusader's Union, used to have an annual sports day with young men coming from all over the country. I had done well in athletics at school and decided to show these Christians a thing or two. Night after night in the summer weeks I trained on the running track to bring my times down. When the great day came, I won both the 100 yards and the 440 yards, if I remember rightly. That set me going. A man

I met while training offered to coach me. I joined his club, and every Saturday found me taking part in one athletic meeting or another. Here, too, I dreamed of performances of high distinction. As I know now, there was never any chance of that, but a fellow can dream, can't he? This, too, was taking precedence over Jesus Christ, though in themselves there was nothing wrong with these two things.

As you can imagine, the Lord was not content to occupy third place in my life. Again and again He spoke to me. I never went into a meeting of any spiritual power without His pointing at these two things, and I was deeply troubled. I was following them so intensely that I knew it would never be enough merely to demote them in my system of priorities; if Jesus was really to be Lord, they would have to go altogether.

At that time the Crusader Bible class I was attending held a Senior Sunday, when the usual leaders gave the conduct of the meeting over to some of the senior boys. I was asked to give one of the two addresses. Without much thought I agreed. It was only afterward that I realized that I had promised to speak for Christ while this controversy was still unresolved. Night after night when I came home from the bank I went to my room to fight out the battle with Sunday coming nearer. I knew I could not speak for Him without being willing to give up these two things. But how could I withdraw from both orchestra and the athletics club when friends had spent so much time on me? In any case, I did not want to lay my teen-age dreams and idols in the dust. At this distance these two interests, with my achievements virtually nil, seem pathetically trivial; but the issue was a big one: who was going to be lord?

Up to that time I had been a stammerer, so much so that my widowed mother had once taken me to a Christian Science practitioner. But Christian Science provided little help. As I grew older, the stammering had moderated somewhat, but it was still there. This might have posed problems for me in public speaking, but I had forgotten about the stammer in my preoccupation with the bigger issue I was facing.

Then the Lord seemed to draw back the veil of the future and showed me vistas of service for Him, souls being won, other lives being changed, His kingdom being extended; on and on into the distance I saw it stretching. Then He said, "All this and more, if you are prepared to 'lay in dust life's glory dead' at My feet!'" Miss this for the sake of paltry baubles? That night I "counted all things but loss for the excellency of the knowledge of Christ Jesus my Lord."

The surrender was made, letters of resignation were written, and I went forward with Jesus to speak the message He gave me. For the first time, I experienced the Holy Spirit anointing with power my words to convey His message to other hearts. Afterward I realized I had not stammered—and I have not since. Jesus had delivered me.

I have so far skipped over the events immediately following my conversion at Southwold, because my first receiving of Christ was incomplete until I had acknowledged His lordship over me on those specific issues.

I must now go back and recount my first experiences as they happened on my Calvary road. I returned home almost dazed from the holiday houseparty. I had been made new; I found I had a new awareness of that spiritual realm of which I had been oblivious. Then, too, I had a new outlook; the "things of the world"—that is, the prizes and pleasures that everybody else was pursuing so ardently—had lost their attraction for me. More than that, I had received a whole new range of appetites that could be satisfied only with heavenly food.

It was this last which posed problems for me, because I found myself completely alone on this new pilgrimage with little or no means to satisfy these new appetites. I knew no one else in my locality who had received the spiritual birth I had and no place where I could hear again that message that had brought peace to me. More than that, I had just left school and had not yet found a job. So I sat around at home, reading my Bible and the few Christian books I had acquired and paradoxically feeling miserable, in spite of my joy in the Lord. It did not occur to me that some churches might be preaching this message.

Like many a new Christian, I thought that the only ones who preached the message I needed were those in the circles from whom I had first heard it. What I had received seemed to bear no relation to what I had heard in school chapel when I was being confirmed. It was natural, therefore, to seek to find the fellowship and help I needed in some movement parallel to that which had led me to Jesus Christ. I found it in the Crusaders' Union. This is a union of Bible classes for schoolboys scattered across Britain, interdenominational in character and unconnected with any particular church, and aimed to cater spiritually to school-aged youth of the middle classes, a segment of the population often unreached with the gospel. The founders of this and similar movements, without recognizing for a moment any class distinction in the body of Christ, nonetheless aimed to infiltrate this neglected social strata—and how glad I am they did, for our family was not likely ever to be affected by anything that might go on in the churches.

When, after some time of walking alone, I learned that there was a Crusader Bible class in our district, I determined to go. But it was not easy to overcome my natural reserve and turn up one Sunday afternoon, unknown and unannounced, and tell them I had come because Jesus had become my Savior. Only the urge of a new life within made me do it. The meeting itself was not impressive nor the speaker especially gifted, but it was the same message I had heard months ago in Southwold, and it was a draught of cool water to a thirsty man.

Thereafter Crusaders became my spiritual milieu. Here I found the spiritual warmth and fellowship I needed, and in Crusaders there was laid the foundation of that attitude to the Scriptures which has dominated me ever since. Here I gained my first experience in Christian service. I am always a little embarrassed when, as I travel the world now with the gospel, I am asked my denomination. The fact is that all my spiritual development has come outside the churches. We in Crusaders went to church, of course, but it was difficult to find in our area churches that were Bible-based, and we never became deeply integrated in them. We found our growth in fellowship one with another. Even when I was called to full-time service later on, it was with a movement which, though very much serving the churches, did so from an interdenominational stance.

Here I think I should pause to explain something of the spiritual situation in England and the important part that interdenominational movements have played. In North America there is no lack of whole denominations which are solidly evangelical. In addition there are any number of independent churches equally Bible-based. Not so in England; there is not one principle denomination which can claim to be clearly evangelical throughout; every denomination is infected either with traditionalism or liberalism, or with both. There is, however, in every denomination a "remnant according to the election of grace," both ministers and people, and they have raised up individual churches in the denominations which present a scriptural message and have witnessed a work of the Holy Spirit in their midst. They stand as beacon lights in our country. But had God not raised up such interdenominational agencies as the Children's Special Service Mission, the Scripture Union, the Crusaders Union, Inter-Varsity Fellowship, the Keswick Convention, and many others in order to present His gospel, whole sections of recent generations would never have heard. But He has indeed raised up these movements and a host have, as a result, found life in Christ. And the strange thing is that, although all these agencies have operated outside the denominations and without relation to them, they have fed back much of their spiritual life into the churches.

Some of Britain's most noted Christian leaders who have ministered within the denominations would never have heard the message of the gospel nor developed in Christ but for these interdenominational movements. Such men as John Stott, Alan Redpath, Tom Rees, and others are known now on both sides of the Atlantic. This process has gone on to such an extent that now the spiritual situation in Britain is very different from what it was when I was finding my feet as a Christian in the 1920s and 1930s, and the evangelical movement has become infinitely stronger. Increasing numbers of truly converted men have been entering the ministry of the various denominations and through them a growing company of young and old have been turning to the Lord, so that the denominations, liberal as they still may be in the main, have had to acknowledge the new life within their borders.

In my case it was among the Crusaders Union of Bible classes that I found the fellowship and biblical foundation I needed. I must not give the impression that all I did was to sit as a Christian teen-ager, piously listening to Bible messages on Sunday afternoons. In that part of northwest London, Crusader classes were, one might say, "thick on the ground." In all the adjoining suburbs there were similar classes served by devoted laymen. As a result, a great crop of senior boys had become Christians and were hungry for God. These young men in their late teens and early twenties, the fruit of these neighboring classes, gathered together into a fellowship that met regularly. Most of us were starting work in offices and the like in the City of London and needed one another. To use the words of Scripture, we "provoked one another to love and good works," and we moved together in our spiritual development.

As I began work in a London bank, the little Crusader badge I wore in the lapel of my jacket was especially precious to me. Although the world did not know what that little badge meant, I knew, and God knew. It meant that I was marked out by Jesus to be separated from the world, part of a special people unto Himself. Separation from the world was no hardship to me—it was the cause of a secret joy, to be no more of the world, even as He was not of the world. Crusader badges proliferated in the City of London as young people came from the surrounding suburbs to work there, and we all recognized one another and knew we were all in possession of the same secret joy. Lunch hours in city restaurants were often times of joyous Christian fellowship.

Three

Early Lessons

THE EARLY DAYS of our Christian lives are immensely important. They are the formative years from which the rest of our spiritual experience will develop. God knows the end from the beginning; as the divine Potter, He knows what He is fashioning out of the clay. Each successive stage of the moulding is part of the whole process. Nothing is haphazard, without significance. The ultimate vessel is the product of all that has gone before; every previous stage in its shaping was necessary. This invests our early years with special significance, and the new Christian should be as open and responsive as he knows how. God has vested interests in him, and he must realize that he is, as Paul was, "a chosen vessel unto Him to bear His name before the Gentiles." The experiences he is going through are the early fashioning of that vessel out of shapeless clay.

The lessons that God teaches us in those early days, therefore, are not only for those days, but are to be constantly applied—indeed they will need to be learned again and again.

I would like to share three such early lessons. They are not given in any chronological order; they are just extracted from that general period which I call my "early days."

The first lesson was that grace puts into us what God wants out of us. That is the only way He will ever get any holiness from us, because there is none there by nature. I came to see

24

this via the back door, that is, by painfully experiencing the very opposite. One day I saw a man walking the streets carrying sandwich boards on which were inscribed texts of Scripture—you know, encouraging ones like "The wicked shall be turned into hell!"

I said to myself, "I think people like that do more harm than good."

A little voice whispered in my heart, "But would you do the same for Me?"

"Yes, I suppose so," I said, "if You really wanted me to."

"All right, then, get boards and carry texts round the streets!"

I was aghast! I couldn't, and I wouldn't. "Then don't expect any more blessing from Me until you do."

I lost all the joy of the Lord and I was in darkness for I cannot remember how long. No more blessing from God, I felt, until I did this, to me an excruciatingly difficult thing!

At last the Lord met me in my misery. I cannot remember what He used, but ultimately I said to myself, "I am miserable, but who is making me miserable? Does God make His children miserable? Of course not! Then who is making me miserable?"

It came to me it could only be Satan. That little voice I heard was not the voice of God, but Satan simulating God's voice. Jesus had said that the devil was a liar, and what I had been listening to and believing was a lie. In that moment I was free from my bondage and rejoicing in the Lord again.

"Lord," I said, "I've learned something today; and I think I'll recognize that voice when Satan challenges me to do things You have not put in me; and on principle, I am not going to do them. I hope I shan't make a mistake, Lord, and excuse myself from things You obviously want me to do. But surely I can trust You to put into me what You want out of me, so that I have the inner desire and a joy in doing it."

The interesting thing is that God did just that in the same sort of matter. Years later, I was part of a team of students conducting a mission in a working-class parish. We wanted to stir up the district and make them know that something was on. We obtained a lorry, on which we put a huge poster, "War declared on Public Enemy Number 1, that old serpent, the

devil." We climbed aboard and drove around the parish singing gospel choruses and announcing the meetings with glad-
ness in our hearts and joy on our faces. No painful compunction
here—we wanted to do it and we were doing so with Jesus. I
am sure the Lord used our joyful testimony.

I began, then, to learn that I could trust Jesus to put into me
what He wanted out of me, and that if I found Him asking of me
what was not in me, then I could confess that fact to Him and
offer myself a candidate for Him to work in me "that which was
well-pleasing in His sight."

It is difficult to summarize in a sentence the second lesson
from those early days, but the incident will speak for itself. I
began attending regularly the Crusader fellowship meeting
already referred to, through which God blessed me deeply.
After a time I was invited to become the secretary of this
gathering. I was thrilled to be asked and immediately said yes.
In the days that followed I felt increasingly uneasy, because the
real reason I had accepted so readily was pride. I got no peace
until I had written to one of the leaders to say that, for reasons I
did not care to go into in a letter, I could not go forward with the
proposal and must withdraw. The older Christian, a saintly
man of deep experience, came to see me and dug out of me why
I would not go forward. I had to tell him, and I added, "If I can't
do this without pride, then obviously I must not do it."

"Then the job will not be done," he answered, "at least, not
by you. If you continue on that basis, there is nothing that you
will be able to do for the Lord. And that is exactly what the
devil intends, and the work of the Lord to that degree will be
halted. That is why Satan provoked you to pride in the first
place.

"The answer is," he continued, "to do it nonetheless—but
without pride. And if you ask how, simply confess to Jesus
whenever Satan makes you proud, and He will forgive the sin
and cleanse you from its stain—and you keep right on with the
service He has given you. If Satan brings pride again, then go
again to Jesus, and He will cleanse you again—but don't let
Satan deter you from doing what God calls you to do."

How often I have needed to apply that lesson!

Yet another lesson related to the matter of soulwinning. What a terrible word! It is, after all, a technical term used only among Christians, like that other word, *witnessing*. Such terms are quite unknown to ordinary worldly people. The initiated eventually discover that soulwinning and witnessing are something Christians are supposed to do; but as they do not often succeed in doing them, the words only threaten them. At least, that is what the word *soulwinning* did to me. Although I knew I was saved by grace, I felt that I hardly had the right to call myself a Christian until I had won at least one soul to Christ; and therefore, did I try! I talked to different people at the office, but the result was only argument. Everybody loves an argument about religion, and that is all I seemed to provoke. There was not the first sign of anyone turning his life over to Jesus Christ. I had to learn that I was trying too hard, that the work of begetting men anew was not my work but the Lord's.

Along with trying too hard, I was afraid that if I did succeed in winning anyone for the Lord, I would be personally and intimately involved with him afterward. I feared I would not have enough to give them and that my own spiritual poverty would soon be revealed. I had read of Christians who had given a tract to someone in a railway carriage, talked to him, got him to make a decision for Christ, and said goodbye to him, never to see him again. That was the sort of soulwinning I wanted—not to continue to give myself to that person afterward.

At last I turned the matter of winning others over to the Lord Jesus, and then it began to happen. I was surprised how little I had to do—He was doing it, not I. At the Crusader Bible class I had joined after my conversion, I heard them praying for a young fellow who came only occasionally and seemed indifferent to the gospel. Hearing him prayed-for so often, I called on him one day and asked if he would come with me to some special evangelistic meetings in the district. We went together several times; then one day he said to me, "Last night when I got home from the meeting, I asked God to make me a Christian."

It had happened at last, and I seemed to have done so little. More than that, the very thing I had feared happened too. My mother was going away on holiday while I would be at work in the City of London. The question of where to stay in her absence was resolved when my friend's parents asked me to stay with them. For two weeks this new Christian and I were thrown together; I had to share the little I knew of Jesus with him, and we were made deeply one in Christian love and became closely associated afterward.

This began to happen again and then again. At the hockey club in which I used to play, another team member and I were given a lift home after a match. He seemed the kind of person who would have little interest in the things of God. Yet, when he saw the book I was carrying, *The Life of George Whitefield,* he asked me if I was interested in Christianity. I told him I most certainly was and that Christ was becoming the whole of my life. He then told me how he had been searching for spiritual reality for a long time, that he had been going to ministers and reading books, all to no avail. Sitting in the back of the car, I told him that I had begun much further back than he and yet Jesus had found me.

As this team member listened he became quite excited. I arranged for him to come around to my home, and it was easy that night to show him the way of salvation and lead him to Christ. He in turn told a friend of his, who like him had been searching for God, and he, too, a few weeks later turned his life over to Christ in the same sitting room.

So it went on. I was overjoyed that what had seemed so impossible was beginning to happen, and that not by my own doing, but rather the Lord's. I said, "If this can go on happening, then I don't want to live for anything else."

> 'Tis worth living for this
> To administer bliss
> And salvation in Jesus' Name.

I felt that to "count all things, but loss for Christ" was a small price. Yet it was not by paying a price that these things began to happen, but rather by ceasing to try to do God's work for Him and *expecting* Him to lead me to those in whom He was working. I came to see that I could not help anyone to find the Lord except those who wanted to, and the causing them to want to—by far the greater part—was wholly His work. "No man can come unto Me except the Father which sent Me draw him."

Four

Spiritual Development

I HAVE SAID THAT the whole crowd of us young men from the Crusader classes of northwest London moved together in our spiritual development. As I look back, I see three phases of such development, and as I was deeply involved and they became the foundation of so much else for me, I must share them.

First, there grew up in us a great eagerness to study the Word of God and a tremendous veneration for it. Although we were only in our late teens and early twenties, we devoured everything we could on scriptural truths, no matter how solid and heavy the book might be. We were especially influenced by the works of E. W. Bullinger with his emphasis on "rightly dividing the word of truth," which for him meant making a clear distinction between the kingdom and the church. As we followed his line, the Bible opened up as a coherent whole and made sense as it never had before. Each of us loved to dig into the Scriptures on our own, getting to the meaning of every phrase and nuance of expression and trying to find the original behind the English translation.

Each day as I traveled on the London Underground to the bank where I worked, I did so with my Bible and notebook—the Bible discreetly disguised so that I could work on it without attracting too much attention in the crowded carriages. Very often the lunch hour would be spent likewise, studying and making notes in a quiet corner of a city restaurant, except when a group of us had a lunch together for fellowship. I tried to set aside one night a week to continue digging into the Word. The Epistle to the Romans was a very special object of study, so much so that it became something of a joke with my mother.

"You're always studying Romans," she used to say. "Whenever you come with a new book I know before I look, it's a book on Romans!"

I was not unique in this preoccupation with the Bible; we were all moving together. I knew I was preparing myself for future service, and that gave added incentive. I never for one moment thought it would be full-time service; the most I wanted was to be an adequate Bible class leader, or some such. And though I have ministered all over the world for forty years since then, I have had no other Bible training than what I received on the London Underground, in city restaurants, in the quietness of my bedroom, and of course, in the rough and tumble of ministering the Word since than, where I have been, as it were, trained on the job.

I am innocent of theological training as usually understood, but I do not feel this a disadvantage. I have had to work on the sacred text directly, and there is no theological teacher like the Holy Spirit Himself. However, I would dearly love to have acquired some knowledge of the original languages of that text, Hebrew and Greek, but my precious Young's *Analytical Concordance*, which travels with me almost everywhere, has gone some way to make good that deficiency.

There were, however, dangers in pursuing the line of things we did. We venerated the Scriptures so much that we had no vision for the winning of the lost. "The Word will do its own work if we just preach it," we used to say; but sometimes what we preached was quite inappropriate to the needs of the hapless boys who listened to us, and there was no urgency in what we had to give. Then, too, we began to graduate from Bullinger to other writers who had each taken his ideas one step further, until eventually we found ourselves in the arid desert of extreme dispensationalism and flirting with dangerous errors. This caused quite a crisis in the Crusaders Union and we knew we had to stop.

God then led us into the next phase of our development—evangelism. I hate to use that term, as it sounds technical and mechanical and is so bandied about in ecclesiastical circles that it often ends up only as an item on the agenda of a committee meeting. But there was nothing technical or mechanical about what happened to us. God aroused us from our preoccupation with doctrine, giving us a concern for those who did not know Christ and an expectancy that He would actually save them there and then.

This concern and expectancy came about by the coming into our circle of Tom Rees. In later years he was to become one of Britain's outstanding evangelists and held some of the largest and most fruitful campaigns in Britain right up to his death in 1970. But at this time he had just begun and was quite unknown, being only in his early twenties. He had given up his job and, relying financially on God from day to day, was going around the country on a motorbike in a "dirty pair of gray bags" (the casual wear of those days), preaching the gospel, full of humor, song, and spiritual passion—a cheerful troubadour of Jesus Christ, if ever there was one.

Although we were then so different from Tom in outlook, he was quite irresistible and we fell in love with him. He came to conduct evangelistic meetings in some of our classes; we heard a preaching of the gospel such as we never had before and felt the Holy Spirit's blessing in a way that was quite new to us. There was no question of trying not to let our minds wander as he spoke—we could not think of anything else even if we tried to. People were gripped and surrendered to Christ all around us—something we had not really expected till then. We all caught fire and began to pray and expect young people to turn to Christ—and they did so in all our classes and wherever we began to preach.

Then Ian Thomas came into the picture. He is now known as Major Ian Thomas and has had a fruitful ministry all over the world, having established his Torchbearers centers in a number of countries. But then he was simply a member of a nearby Crusader class and had just left school to start as a medical student in a London hospital. He, too, caught fire, as was quite apparent by his very countenance—Tom Rees used to call him the "glow-worm." None of us could have dreamed what ministry to the world was going to emanate from the small beginnings of those days.

It was about this time I began to run my own Crusader class in a nearby residential district called the Hampstead Garden Suburb. It was a landmark for me, as I now can see it was a training ground for future service. It came about in this way:

While I was plodding away at a rather dreary nine-to-five job in a London bank, my brother Brian was having the time of his life at Cambridge University, being deeply involved in the Christian Union there. The Cambridge Inter-collegiate Christian Union is the oldest and largest of all the Inter-Varsity Christian Unions in Great Britain, and it has a famous history. The Christian activities Brian took part in during term-time were endless, and in the vacations it was one long round of camps, student missions, and the like. I envied the life he led, compared with my daily commuting to a city office. But it was what I needed, and the Lord used the very lack of excitement to lead me deeper into His Word.

Then my brother, always full of drive, planned a ten-day compaign for young people in the Hampstead Garden Suburb and gathered an outstanding team of university students, some of whom were later to achieve undreamed-of distinction. One was a reserved, studious young man named Donald Coggan who, being an excellent musician, was cast in the role of pianist for the team. Today Donald is the Archbishop of Canterbury, the Primate of the whole Anglican Church throughout the world, and a noted evangelical, listened to with respect throughout Great Britain and beyond. None of us could have conceived that God would call him to such an office and such a task. He was not even headed for the ministry, but was simply planning to lecture in Hebrew and Syriac in an academic post. I always remember him as the first pianist I ever heard "swing" gospel choruses, and he spoiled me for anything but this free, extempore style of playing for evangelistic work.

Many young people found Christ as their Savior, and as a result a regular Sunday afternoon class for school boys and girls was started. When my brother and the team went back to Cambridge, it was left to me to carry on the class. I divided it into two, boys and girls, and affiliated them to the Crusaders Union. With the help of Alastair Wallace, likewise in a city office, who had himself been converted in the campaign, I proceeded to give it all I had.

Alastair and I labored for those sixty or seventy boys as any pastor might labor for his church. My job in the bank was completely incidental to the work for these boys. There was every boy to pray for, the address for the main meeting on Sunday afternoons to prepare, new boys to hunt up, and lapsed members to visit. There were games and activities to arrange, camps to organize and, most demanding of all sometimes, the "keenites" meetings to lead. We called these "keenites" because they were the boys who were keen, that is, had been converted. Here we got down to the Word more deeply, and I remember taking a series with them once when we attempted to cover one book of the Bible each week. As a young Christian myself, it took almost every waking moment, office hours apart, to cover the ground and get the study ready.

I little knew what bearing this would have on future service; I was just doing what God gave me to do and loving it. But in this new life in Christ, the simplest tasks for today are full of tremendous possibilities for tomorrow; therefore "whatsoever thy hand findeth to do, do it with all thy might."

The third stage of our development was quite the most important and transformed life for us all. I can only recount this through my own experience.

I have kept a diary for one short period of my life only, and I have the tattered pages before me as I write. Under Tuesday, August 28, 1934 (I was twenty-six), I wrote:

> Have had much temptation from "self"—envy, jealousy, self-glory, vain imagining. This morning I claimed Galatians 2:20. The Lord has delivered me from self— praise His Name! I am standing on the promises of God!

This is the story behind those words. I had just returned from a Crusader camp where I had been an "officer" in charge of a tent of boys. There I saw other tent "officers" being much more used by God among the boys than I was, and I found jealousy in my heart. I wrestled with it, but it refused to lie down! I knew that when I got home and had more time, I would have to face this out with God.

One morning God led me to the words, "I have been crucified with Christ . . . it is no longer I that live but Christ that
liveth in me" (Gal. 2:20). I saw that my trouble was "I" trouble:
I was an "I" specialist. I also saw that God had done something
about this. I was reading the verse in the Revised Version,
where it is "I have been crucified" rather than "I am crucified"
as in the King James Version. That seemed to suggest that Paul
was not professing an experience of crucifixion so much as
pointing back to an historic fact in which he was involved and
on which he was counting.

Then I understood: Roy Hession, the man whose center was
self, had been judged and crucified with Christ nineteen hundred years before. I was therefore to see myself ended, not
mended; and instead of struggling with self, I was to accept the
sentence of death pronounced so many years ago and trust God
progressively to carry out the execution. This meant for me the
end of trying to live by my own efforts, which till then had been
the basis of my Christian life. More important, I then saw that
the Lord Jesus was the source of the new life that had to be
lived, for the verse went on to say, "it is no longer I that live,
but Christ that liveth in me."

I had been reading one or two books by Norman Grubb, in
which he showed that faith was not asking for what you had not
got, but making use of what you had; that if God said you had it,
then you had to believe it and thank Him for it; and that if the
promise was to be made good in experience, you had to add the
word of faith and declare you had received it, quite apart from
feelings. That morning I believed the Word of God, that for me
"self" was on the cross and Jesus on the throne, my throne
which was now His; and I knew that I would need to add,
sometime, somehow, the word of faith in regard to this new
relationship into which I had entered.

The opportunity came when I was taking the chair of the
fellowship meeting for senior Crusaders. In opening that meeting I recounted my struggles with self and acknowledged the
new relationship with Jesus which I had entered by faith.
Immediately after, Ian Thomas rushed up to me with a shining
face to tell me that the same thing had happened to him. He
had been having the same struggles, and God had met him
through a booklet called "The Life that Wins" by Charles G.

Trumbull, which emphasized that the resources of the Christian life are not prayer, Bible study, fellowship, worship, service, and so on, but just Jesus Christ Himself. Ian had seen it—there is only one life that wins, and that is Christ's. It was not only that our lives were Christ's, but much more important, Christ was now our life. We saw this as being filled with the Spirit.

As I began to count on this in faith and praise God for it, so much of the striving that had characterized me fell away, and the Lord Jesus began to do through me things I had never seen Him do before. People began to be saved with an ease that astonished me, not through effort on my part, but simply as the result of faith in Christ.

Ian and I were especially drawn together in this new vision. Soon the Lord dealt similarly with others of our group, filling us with His Holy Spirit, and there was quite a little revival among us. It was then that Alan Redpath, who worked as a chartered accountant with the Imperial Chemical Industries and lived in the same area, came across our path. The Lord taught him the same simple truth, and life became new for him. In the years since then, God has given him a mighty pastoral, evangelistic, and "deeper life" ministry all over the world. But then he was but a babe in Christ; he had just returned to the Lord after years of backsliding and was giving his first faltering messages in a tiny mission hall in the district. None of us guessed—least of all himself—what God would make of him in coming days. We were simply a band of young men and women, all moving together and rejoicing over new discoveries of the riches of Christ.

Ian Thomas, inspired by the example of Tom Rees, now felt guided by God to give up his medical studies and career to go out to do the work of an evangelist, without any financial resources save faith. He went like a flame of fire from place to place as doors opened for him. He seemed so young, yet had the most unusual ability to preach the Word, leaving everywhere a trail of salvation behind him. For him, as for us all, faith was the victory that overcame the world. I remember the times of prayer he and I spent together, when we prayed the most extraordinary prayers of faith, utterly confident that Jesus was on the throne and the devil on the run; and so we found it in experience. We were on tiptoe with expectancy, not knowing what God was going to do next, or what He would ask of us.

Tom and Ian, then, were having great experiences in "the high places of the field," preaching the gospel in place after place, although they were still only in their early days. The reports of their campaigns and meetings in their periodical prayer letters always made my heart leap and my pulse beat faster. Then they began to say to me, "You ought to leave the bank and be out with us, preaching the gospel."

"Don't tempt me," I said. "There's nothing I would love to do more; but I have prayed prayers for the boys of my Crusader class which have not yet been answered, and I must stay until they are."

"Well," they said, "we'll pray you out."

God was soon to answer their prayers, but in a way none of us ever expected. It came about by a God of grace "bailing me out" of a serious mess I got myself into. That is the next stage of my journey along my Calvary road.

Five

By-Path Meadow and Back

THERE WAS AS I have said, an air of expectancy among the young Christians of those days which spread far beyond my own immediate circle. There were a number of contributing factors. First of all, there appeared Norman Grubb's biography of C. T. Studd, the famous English cricketer of the generation before, who at the call of God had given away a huge inherited fortune to be a missionary, first in China, then in India, and latterly and more extensively, in the heart of Africa, trusting God as a poor man for all his needs. He became the founder of the Worldwide Evangelization Crusade, all of whose workers seemed to us to have the same dare-devil spirit of dedication. This book shook young Christians out of their complacency all over the country and gave them a vision of greater things.

Then came Edwin Orr. He is known in Christian circles all over the English-speaking world as a distinguished historian of revivals and has written a number of scholarly works on the subject. But at that time he was just a young fellow, barely out of his teens, who was so imbued with the vision of revival that he gave up his job in Northern Ireland and took to the roads on his bicycle with but a few shillings in his pocket, calling on Christians all over Great Britain to pray for revival. As he ministered, a spirit of repentance became apparent, while his daily needs were supplied in the most unusual ways. He recounted his experiences in a book, *Can God?* which was

devoured by eager young Christians everywhere. He undertook tour after tour in other countries, with a book of his
experiences appearing after each tour, keenly awaited by a
growing public. When he returned from his tour in Australia, a
huge crowd filled one of London's largest halls with most of the
evangelical leaders in attendance to welcome this stripling
home, and he spoke with an authority which searched many
hearts. Quite extraordinary!

Then, as already mentioned, there were Ian Thomas and
Tom Rees, equally young and equally daring in their faith.

The result of all this was that others of us could not but
feel that if these men could venture forth, why not the rest
of us?

It can be seen with hindsight that, in a situation of such
enthusiasm and expectancy, it would be easy for Satan to
transform himself into an angel of light and lead us away from
our true center into some by-path meadow. This is exactly what
Satan did, at least in the circle of which I was a part. But God
overruled and brought good out of it. I for one was led as a
result into full-time service and given a ministry which has
continued ever since. Such is God's grace that, once things go
wrong, the only thing He is concerned with is recovery, and
recover us all He certainly did. This diversion happened as
follows.

In northwest London we had begun monthly weekend ral-
lies to follow up the campaigns of Tom Rees, Saturday night for
the Christians and Sunday night after church for the non-
Christians. With the spiritual tide rising, we were anxious that
each weekend should take us further than the previous one.
We were careful, therefore, to select speakers who would one
by one present a more radical message than those before and
who would lead us to yet more steps of faith. One of them, I
remember, called us to an extended time of prayer and encouraged us to ask God, in faith, to save a certain number of souls
that weekend. In the event, precisely that number of people
did accept Christ.

In our search for ever more challenging speakers we were
recommended to call somebody from the Bible College of
Wales, near Swansea, about which we had heard things that
made our ears tingle—a story of faith attempting and ac-

complishing the impossible. It had been started by a Welshman, Rees Howells, who had been saved in the Welsh revival years before and about whom there was always something of the mystique of that revival. He had certainly had some remarkable experiences of being used by God, similar to that movement from which he had emerged. He had had the vision of setting up a new Bible college to train young men and women for the mission field, and both he and those associated with him had breath-taking stories to tell of acquiring properties with nothing but the promises of God to depend upon.

So we invited one of Howell's associates to come to us, and his ministry certainly seemed to be in great power. He astonished us by saying that God had revealed to Rees Howells that He was going to complete the evangelization of the world in the next thirty years through the college, if he, like Abraham, would "against hope believe in hope." It came to be known as the "Every Creature Vision." In the next thirty years ten thousand young people would pass through the college and out to the mission fields of the world, and vast new premises would be added to make this possible.

The more I heard, the more I felt, "If all this is true, then it is the biggest thing since Pentecost and I can't afford to be out of it." One of the main things which students were to learn there was how to live by faith and take the supply for their needs out of God's treasury. Giving away all our money (how else could one live by faith if one still had reserves of one's own?) was no problem to us. What was money anyway to young people? In any case, we all held our futures very lightly. For young people to respond to the most costly calls does not necessarily indicate spiritual depth: they are young, they will not run out of life for a long time yet, they are without the responsibility of wife or children, and the call to high adventure is immensely appealing. There was every incentive to "fling the world away and go crusading," and that is how we were caught.

At this point we were not at all thinking of giving everything up and joining the college, but we were highly interested in it and thirsted to hear more. Indeed, I was so affected by the challenge of what I had heard that I felt I should part with the capital that had come to me when my father died and give it to

God—in this instance, to the college. I had some reservations at first about doing this, because the capital had only come to me because my father died without completing a will; otherwise it would have gone to my mother. Ultimately I gave orders to sell half the investments, but carried the transfers in my pocket for days. I finally signed them and then sent the money off—to the horror of my mother when she heard it, but to shouts of praises from the college, who had been praying for just some such sum.

Although we had never been there, we had all become fascinated with the college. It was not surprising, then, that when we heard there was to be a residential conference at the college, about six of us decided to go, including my close friend, Roy Cattell, the leader of a neighboring Crusader class, and one or two lady Crusader leaders.

Rees Howells and the college fulfilled all our expectations. We were quite swept off our feet, and there was nothing I wanted to do more than to be part of it. When Rees Howells told Roy Cattell and me that the Holy Spirit had revealed to him that we were to come to the college, then go to Japan, and that we were to lead the way for five hundred other Crusaders over the next thirty years, and that our names would go down like those of Hudson Taylor, William Carey, and so on, we were finished. How could we say no to such grace as this? When in the meetings the great appeal was made, we went forward with others to hand over our lives, making whatever surrender one does make on such occasions and finding whatever texts one does find in order to persuade oneself one has a call. The truth was, of course, we had been fascinated and caught by the wiles of our own hearts and at all costs we wanted to go.

The whole group of us returned to announce that God had called us to the Bible College of Wales and the mission field, and we all promptly gave up our jobs. There was a great rally of senior Crusaders and others when we each told our story, and we made a profound impression. All sorts of young people were asking themselves whether they should make a like surrender. It was not difficult to see that, because we were each in positions of leadership, many others would follow us. Alan Redpath and his wife, who in the deep sincerity of their hearts were always ready for anything, were greatly impressed and were "teetering on the brink."

The significant thing was, however, that when our decision was made known, the warning lights began to flash in the hearts of many Christians of experience. The central committee of the Crusaders Union had us up before them to give an account of ourselves, for they feared there would be a landslide in the same direction and they expressed their grave misgivings. But we dismissed all such counsel on the ground that it came from people who, we told ourselves, were not willing to pay the price: they had means and possessions of their own, whereas we were giving ours all away.

It did disturb us a bit, however, when these warning lights kept on flashing in increasing numbers, sometimes from very dear older friends. But we felt we could only dismiss what they said on the same ground. Then, when both Tom Rees and Edwin Orr separately expressed the same misgivings and went to great lengths to counsel us to quit this path altogether, we had to stop and open our minds. As we listened to those who had carefully investigated the subject, we had to admit that error had crept into the teaching of the college through an excess of zeal and that the "Every Creature Vision" was really the hallucination of an overeager mind.

We fought against such conclusions as long as we could, for we hated to see our castles in the air crumble. But at last we had to confess that we had been misled by our own hearts and our desire for the heroic, and not called by the Holy Spirit at all. Thus we all withdrew from the college and gave up our intention to go forward. Not to have done so would have been sheer pride and disobedience on our part, and it would doubtless have led to spiritual disaster. One of our number, a lady Crusader leader, had actually sent her trunk and luggage ahead of her to the college, so narrowly was she saved from catastrophe.

This disillusionment, when like the prodigal son I "came to myself," took place during the time when I had to work a month's notice at the bank before I actually left it. The whole experience was a traumatic one indeed, a true case of a "corn of wheat falling into the ground and dying." First, there was the humiliation of having to admit I was wrong when I had made my brave new decision so public. In "one fell swoop" I lost my reputation in the eyes of everybody. Then, I found that having given my notice to the bank, there was no chance of getting that job back because it had been offered to another. Then, too, it meant giving up what was more precious than anything else to me, the leadership of the Crusader class I had started. My mother, thinking I was "going off to Timbuctoo," felt she could not remain in our London home alone and had given it up in order to live near my brother who was a vicar in a country town right outside London. Thus, when I had finished working my four weeks' notice, I had no other option than to join her in the country and leave the class of boys for whose salvation I had labored so hard.

What to do next I did not know. I certainly knew I was not to go to the Bible College in Wales. I could possibly have tried to get a job again in the City of London, and that might not have been too difficult, as I had friends who were anxious to see me established again in ordinary life and they could well have opened some doors. But I felt that God had allowed me to go as far as I had and that I should not hasten back too quickly to a city office. I thought that perhaps the "call" to go to Japan or some other mission field might still be valid. And so I just waited in my mother's home. She was only too glad to see me "restored to my senses," as she put it, whether or not I was actually working.

I was glad of a time of waiting. I had been spiritually and emotionally torn apart by what I had been through, and I needed to be rehabilitated. This rehabilitation came to me as I read the two volumes of the *Life of Hudson Taylor*, the founder of the China Inland Mission, written by Dr. and Mrs. Howard Taylor. It was a relief to forget my own affairs and to lose myself in the details of another person's life and see God's dealings with him. I found it not only utterly absorbing, but Jesus came again to me through its pages, especially as I read the famous chapter, "The Exchanged Life." In it Hudson Taylor tells how he exchanged his own life of self-effort and failure to allow Christ to live His life in him.

That is what I had discovered in August the previous year and which had been, in the months that followed, such a rich experience. But I had got away from it; I had "sought great things for myself" and had entertained the thought of being called to be someone special, different from the run-of-the-mill Christians (terrible expression!). I had been led and deceived by my personal wishes, and I had got into by-path meadow. But as I read those two volumes, I saw Jesus again as the Vine and I but the branch, no one special, very much a run-of-the-mill Christian, and a failing one at that; and I returned to my rest, from which I should never have departed.

As I did so, the mists cleared and I knew for certain that the foreign mission field was not God's place for me. That supposed "call" had come only through the Bible College of Wales and I had clearly to regard my involvement there as a product of my own desires and therefore suspect.

Then an old longing reappeared, not to be back at Crusader work, but to be an evangelist, as were Tom Rees and Ian Thomas. This is what they had prayed for and to which I had immediately responded in my heart, but which I had pushed away because I felt I could never leave my Crusader class. Yet I had been precipitated out of that work and set free from my secular job in a way I had never expected. Now the Lord began to tug my heart toward evangelism at home. This was a "natural" for me, a normal development of what had been happening prior to by-path meadow. God's guidance toward it became simple, quiet, and obvious, so different from the dramatic events that I had thought previously were leading me toward the Bible College of Wales.

During those weeks of waiting in the autumn of 1935, I had written to Ian Thomas telling him of my new conviction, and he arranged for me to participate in an Inter-Varsity student mission at Sheffield, an industrial city in the north of England, in which he was involved. There were a hundred students who were divided into teams of ten each and who conducted simultaneous campaigns in churches all over the city. One of the teams lacked leadership and, much to my disappointment, I was transferred from Ian's to lead this other team. The way in which the Holy Spirit worked through us to bring people to faith in Christ was all the confirmation I could ask that this was what God had called me to. This mission was specially significant in another way, for I met on the team a Welsh girl, a student at Birmingham University, who later became my wife.

But a lot of water had to run under the bridge before I took any notice of her.

I returned home knowing at last God's call for me, and I waited. But nothing happened: "No man hired me." I was hidden away in the country, and there were no calls to preach the gospel. Then I chanced to stay with Alan Redpath (one of those beautiful divine chances), where I heard that the National Young Life Campaign, an interdenominational evangelistic movement among young people, were wanting to appoint young men to their staff. Alan Redpath had felt for quite a time an urgent burden to give up his job as a chartered accountant in order to preach the gospel. We both applied and were accepted and appointed as evangelists, he to work in one part of the country and I in another—just like that!

The National Young Life Campaign had been founded by two brothers—the Brothers Wood, as they were known—who in their youth and without any theological training had stepped out in faith. Fred was the preacher and Arthur the song leader. God's hand was so greatly upon them that for decades they filled the largest halls in Britain, and tens of thousands of young people were converted to Christ. Then, in order to cater for all these young Christians and to lead them further in the work of evangelism, the National Young Life Campaign was founded. "Every campaigner a soulwinner and every church an evangelizing center" was its slogan and aim. Now that the brothers were getting older, they were looking for young men to carry on this work as evangelists, each one to take over an area of the country. They were no more concerned about the formal training of such men than they had been about themselves. All they were looking for were men with a burning desire to preach Christ to young people.

Alan Redpath and I were the first to be appointed under this new development. They took us just as we were, Alan from an accountant's office and me from a bank, with little experience of evangelistic preaching; they gave us the name of their movement to work under, commended us to their circle of friends across the land, and let us loose on the country to preach Christ. This was heady wine indeed for both of us. It mattered not that the stipend for our support was minimal—we would gladly have paid them for the privilege! Neither of us can thank

God enough for the willingness of the Brothers Wood to take the risk and trust us as they did.

So by the grace of God my excursion into by-path meadow was overruled to lead me to the place of God's appointment. I do not regret the money I gave away; it was given to God rather than to man. Nor do I criticize Rees Howells; he was as sincere as he knew how, though mistaken in some things; and, poor man, he ended by losing the confidence of most mission boards who might otherwise have sent their candidates to him for training. My friend, Norman Grubb, has always insisted that he was God's messenger to him for good at a crucial time in his life, and Norman has written his story in a book which has been widely read, *Rees Howells, Intercessor,* from which many people say they have derived much blessing; I am glad. It was doubtless far more my fault than Rees Howells's that I allowed his influence to lead me away from the simplicity that is in Christ.

Nor do I discount the value of the Bible College of Wales now. Since the passing of Rees Howells, the college has quietly dropped the "Every Creature Vision" and become a stable and valuable place of Bible training for young people desiring to prepare themselves for the mission field. I believe the God of grace and forgiveness has a good future for them, as I trust He has for this writer, for all his mistakes. I do not look back on all that has happened with hardness, pointing the finger, but rather with thankfulness to God that through these events He got me to the place where He wanted me, out of a city office and into the work that I have been doing for the past forty years.

Six

The Years of Spring

> The voice of my beloved! Behold, he cometh leaping
> upon the mountains, skipping upon the hills. My beloved
> is like a gazelle, or a young hart: behold, he standeth
> behind our wall, he looketh in at the windows, flourishing
> himself through the lattice. My beloved spake and said
> unto me, "Rise up, my love, my fair one, and come away.
> For, lo, the winter is past, the rain is over and gone; the
> flowers appear on the earth" (Song of Sol. 2:8–12).

IT WAS IN January 1936 that Alan Redpath and I joined the staff
of the National Young Life Campaign and took our first steps in
evangelistic work. We did so having newly entered into the
liberating experience of "Christ in you, the hope of glory." We
had seen that He in us was not only the hope of glory, but the
hope of everything else His work called for. Although we knew
that "in us, that was in our flesh, there dwelt no good thing"
and acknowledged how inexperienced we were, it seemed to
us that by faith in Him who was now our life nothing was
impossible. And so in the name of the Lord we dared to take on
campaign after campaign, even as little David took on the
mighty Goliath. We saw Goliath come down before our eyes
again and again.

For me those early years on the staff of the National Young
Life Campaign were the years of spring, and doubtless Alan
Redpath would say the same for himself. The verses that
precede this chapter describe how it seemed with my soul in

those days. Jesus had come to me, leaping on the mountains, skipping on the hills to announce the coming of spring, the day of grace. But I had been like the girl in the Song of Solomon, cooped up in her hillside cottage, thinking it was still winter— that is, struggling to be a good Christian under the law, striving by my efforts to get what was already mine as gift in Christ, not knowing that I could exchange my life for His. But He had come to call me to dance with Him in the spring of a new life. "Rise up, my love, my fair one, and come away. For lo, the winter is past, the rain is over and gone; the flowers appear on the earth, and the time of the singing of birds is come." I had responded and left my winter cottage, and was leaping with Him on the mountains and skipping with Him upon the hills. Alan and I were to prove the reality of this in the stern field of evangelistic work, each in our different areas of the country, for we were called to a work completely beyond us, that of raising the dead. This was something only God could do, but He by His Spirit dwelt in us to do it. By faith we laid hold of this fact and ventured out in the joy and expectancy of it.

In Britain at that time, the tide was out as far as evengelism was concerned. The country had known in the early nineteen hundreds the mighty crusades of Torrey and Alexander, who had visited our shores from America. They had been followed by the Brothers Wood themselves, who in their youth carried on where Torrey left off and conducted crusades every bit as large and as greatly used by God. But they were older now, and it was some years since they had undertaken such crusades. Gipsy Smith and Lionel Fletcher had been heard throughout the country, but old age had silenced them. More than that, evangelism through the preached word had gone out of fashion, at least, on any wide scale. The open invitation for sinners to turn to Christ was quite unknown, even in evangelical churches.

Yes, the tide was out as far as evangelism was concerned, but that suited us fine, for there was only one way for it to turn and that was in! Alan and I were aware that we were all the time riding a rising tide. In the light of what has happened in Britain in more recent years—the crusades led by Billy Graham and others—our work would appear small today, but it was not so to us. It was marvelous in our eyes, and so it was to the

Christians of those days, who had known so little of a bold, confident evangelism and who had seldom seen souls turning to Christ in any numbers.

In city after city and church after church we conducted the first evangelistic campaigns almost within living memory. This also suited us well, because there were no recent memories of the great work of others to terrify us. The organizers themselves, not having participated in this sort of thing before, did not know whether we were doing it right or wrong—and neither did we sometimes! We moved in the joy of holy confidence, knowing that if God were for us, our weak points were no hindrance and our strong points no help, for it was the working of Another in our midst.

In the light of our own recent experience of Christ, we preached a twofold message: full salvation for the Christian quite as much as an initial salvation for the non-Christian. This was exactly what the widespread membership of the movement needed. The members not only supported their staff evangelists, but themselves came into a new relationship with the Lord and were stimulated to be soulwinners and to engage in their own evangelistic enterprises. A great quickening resulted throughout the movement, and the Holy Spirit gave the gift of the evangelist to any number of young people. It is quite impossible to compute how many were led to Christ as a consequence.

Wherever we went for campaigns, we tried to recruit a team of young people from the local membership of NYLC to assist us. Not only was the part they played—the giving of personal testimonies, the "fishing in" of strangers from the streets, the counseling of seekers, and so on—valuable to the evangelist, but they themselves caught fire, and the local NYLC branch became a soulwinning center as never before. Quite a number of those who helped us on teams were themselves called later into full-time service for the Lord.

Although I was appointed to the Midlands, while Alan Redpath covered London and the South of England, my first months were spent in London where I had a number of engagements to fulfill. Thus the first campaign I took on the staff of the NYLC was a joint one with Alan, helped by a team of campaigners. It was hardly an auspicious start to an evangelistic ministry, being held in a run-down Congregational Church, in a run-down industrial area called, strangely, Gospel Oak, at the first meeting of which there were precisely six persons. But faith cared not whether it was auspicious or not; we were in the joy of spring with Jesus. Here is the report from the prayer letter that I sent to those who were praying for us:

> This church was in a very poor condition—breathing heavily—with a Sunday evening congregation of only about thirty. Numbers were small throughout—we began with six—but they increased as we continued. Many of the regular congregation refused to come after they had heard what our message was really like. The old trouble of "itching ears"! We did not indulge in ear tickling! Whereas our message accounted for the conversion of some, it roused the ire of others. They, including the minister, didn't mind telling us!
>
> However, the Lord brought quite a number of strangers in, and fishing folk in from the streets was quite successful. Almost every night there were souls saved in ones and twos, and some of them were lovely cases. One young woman resisted the Holy Ghost night after night, and we seemed to be unable to get anywhere with her in personal talks. One night the Lord met and mastered her in her room, and the next evening we found her bubbling over with joy in Christ. With great delight she told us that the first sin had already gone—she had chucked her cigarettes away—that's the stuff, sister! "Every sin had to go 'neath the cleansing flow." The testimony meeting on the last night was good and souls were saved then. We had much to praise God for—the team worked and prayed like tigers!

Later in the year I got settled into Birmingham, which is in the heart of the Midlands, the industrial area of England. The National Young Life Campaign had recently taken root there, and in the surrounding churches there was a fine nucleus of young men and girls, ready for anything and waiting for a lead. God drew together a number who were willing to work with me as a team in my evangelistic campaigns, and they did so in a costly and highly effective way. When a campaign I was conducting was within reach, these young people gave up their homes for the period of the campaign (they lasted anything from ten to twenty-three days) and would travel directly from work each day to the scene of action, have a meal together, and then take part in the campaign all evening. They slept in the area without going home and went directly off to work from there day after day. On Sundays they would occupy various pulpits in the district, and we would all come together for a great after-church rally in the evening. Very soon they were all imbued with a new vision of Jesus and of full salvation in Him, and their enthusiasm and faith seemed boundless.

The campaigns we had together were mostly in the Black Country, that rough industrial area between Birmingham and Wolverhampton. From some points of view one could understand its gaining for itself the name "Black Country," but they are a wonderful people who live there, with a culture (and an accent!) all their own, and a warmth and receptivity to the gospel that made it all joy to work among them. In each place where we held campaigns—Saltley, Tipton, Old Hill, Dudley, Wolverhampton—the fire of God fell and many were brought to Christ. For each member of that team those years were the years of spring, as they were for me.

In the team there was a student at Birmingham University who often skipped her studies to join in the battle. It was the same Welsh girl I had met on the student mission in Sheffield. Since then, she had fallen away from the Lord and had only just returned to Him; now she was eager to be as involved as possible in His service. As a result of her extramural activities, Revel Williams failed her degree, but I gained a wife! But not just then; it would be nearly two years before that happened.

The next twelve years I spent working very happily under the banner of the National Young Life Campaign, a movement I came to love. Its members scattered throughout the country made it their business to open doors for us, their staff evangelists, and they loved us and backed us up in every possible way. We developed a method whereby a modest plan for an evangelistic campaign in the minds of but a small NYLC branch could be expanded and set up in such a way as to make it a city-wide campaign with a number of churches participating. During that time I conducted something like 140 full evangelistic campaigns, not only in the Midlands, but all over Britain—in churches, town halls and in the summer months in large tents, the latter being a form of evangelistic work I loved most of all. All this would have been quite impossible had the Lord not taught me how to come to Him continually with my emptiness, despairing of self and letting Him "undertake my All to be."

It would serve no useful purpose simply to catalogue all those campaigns. But it is necessary, for two reasons at least, to give some account of those years of spring. First, the main story of this book is that of the grace of God meeting a needy man's heart in revival. But as Charles G. Finney says, "revival always presupposes a declension"; therefore, to understand what grace did, you must understand the declension that set in. To do so, you must first know something more of those glorious years "when the flowers appeared on the earth, and the time of the singing of birds had come," and when I "leaped on the mountains and skipped on the hills" with the risen Lord. It was said indeed that later I declined from that experience and that, "when I opened to my Beloved, He had withdrawn Himself and was gone." Only by some glimpse of what those former years of spring were actually like can it be seen how desperate my need became.

Second, what the Lord did, He did, and that for His glory, whatever my later experiences of failure and recovery might be. Further experiences of grace do not for a moment invalidate the lessons He taught before. So I shall share briefly what He did and taught then, in the hope that it will still provide challenge and illumination today.

Over the years it was my custom to send to a wide circle of interested friends periodic news and prayer letters in which I gave accounts of the evangelistic work I was doing, as it unfolded month after month. The aim behind those letters was not merely to give reports of Christian work, which can sometimes be dreary, but to do so in such a way as to spur, stimulate, and encourage the reader and to teach him new things. Fortunately, I have preserved copies of most of those news and prayer letters, and they provide the source material for much of this book.

The reading through of fifty years of them has itself been quite a task! This does mean, however, that I do not have to rely on my memory as to what happened in those years, and I can quote selected portions of them, which I trust will give immediacy to the story. More than that, such quotations will show how I saw and interpreted things at the time, rather than how I would see and interpret them now, which in turn means it will give a view of my pilgrimage as it unfolded itself to me. Whereas some real measure of the glory of God will, I hope, be revealed, my own immaturities and superficialities will certainly be exposed to view, and you may not always like what you see, no more than I always do now. But if this is the story of one man's pilgrimage, he should be known as he was at each stage.

Seven

Leaping on the Mountains

THE EVENTS DESCRIBED in the reports that follow are not outstanding beyond the work of any other evangelist. Such signs have always followed the preaching of the gospel of the grace of God; it has always been His instrument for the accomplishment of moral and spiritual miracles. Other preachers of the gospel could match such stories of the triumphs of grace many times over. But I quote these reports because, not only were they an essential part of my pilgrimage, but they confirmed for me that this was indeed the way—living in the resurrection life of Christ and believing for his victory, not merely asking for it.

The prayers with which I and my teammates steeped everything were not merely prayers of asking and pleading, but, above all, prayers of believing, for "what things soever ye desire, when ye pray, believe that ye receive them, and he shall have them." And we not only believed we received them, but we praised God that we had. We were taught of God to live on praising ground in this battle for souls. And as we believed, so it happened. Thus it was we "leaped on the mountains and skipped on the hills"; we were fighting not *for* victory, but *from* it, a victory already accomplished in the cross and rising again of our Lord Jesus Christ.

One of our first campaigns in the Black Country was in the parish church of Old Hill.

31st October to 9th November, 1936, Old Hill Parish Church, near Birmingham. A good solid evangelical church run on spiritual lines. One of the most glorious campaigns I have been on, not because of very big numerical results, but because of wonderful experiences of the power of God that we had as we prayed and fought and because we came out with the conviction as never before that our God is the Rock! Hallelujah and Glory! The campaign was saturated with prayer! We will not soon forget some of those experiences of receiving the promised power from on high! Both Saturday afternoons were spent in prayer, and throughout a number of the meetings the team were in another room praying. They held the devil down while I hit him in the next room! The campaign was noteworthy also because we preached, testified and urged on the Christians the experience of sanctification, death to sin and the filling of the Spirit. The result was overflowing blessing. The testimonies of the team on this experience brought many under conviction! It was indeed an impressive moment when one of the team told how she had got this blessing of the filling of the Spirit only that morning at 3 A.M. after spending hours with the Lord and after she finally consented to put something right in her life. The beginning of the campaign was as sticky and difficult as any I have known. By Monday night we knew of no one blessed or saved. But this only caused us to get lower before the Lord—so the devil overreached himself! How often he falls into the pit he himself has dug! Every night after that people found Christ, even on those occasions when we spoke only to Christians.

Halfway through the campaign I felt led to devote two nights very specially to the Christians and I must say I obeyed reluctantly, thinking I was missing an opportunity with the unconverted. But God set His seal and Christians were convicted of hindrances and really sought the blessing. Sunday night saw a splendid congregation in church and, with the team praying through the service, liberty and power was felt in the pulpit. The call for seekers to walk right up the long aisle to the altar rails was a tremendous test of reality on the part of those who responded, and some four or five bravely knelt at the Communion rails. The first to come was a middle-aged woman. She wept much that night. She said in her testimony next day that she was a Christian before, but that she had come out to receive a "second sprinkling of the precious blood." The testimony meeting on the last night was wonderful and an amazing atmosphere prevailed. Many testified—from small boys to large women! New converts testified brightly, Christians told of blessing received and of the Holy Spirit's filling. There were, too, some moving confessions of sin and hindrance. We went home sorry that it was not to continue another week. Glory to the Lamb alone!

November 10th. St. Paul's Church, Tipton. The day after the campaign! We all felt tired; I felt as dull as ditchwater. I looked up as one of the team was testifying and noticed there were tears in the eyes of some. So I pulled myself together, gave the closing word, and in the personal work afterward six souls were saved and a backslider restored. Glory!

From there we went on to other campaigns in the Black Country, of which the following report can be taken as representative:

9th to 14th January 1937, The People's Mission Hall, Netherton. This was a short campaign in a warm-hearted Black Country church, but though it was only for six days, the Lord gave us (I had the Birmingham team working with me) and abundant harvest. We had wonderful times of prayer, and these Black Country folks packed into the prayer room in good numbers and simply poured out their hearts to God. Every night almost there were souls saved amidst much rejoicing, many of whom had been long prayed for. One night one of the team failed to turn up, and I called at his house on the way home to enquire. He said he had been definitely led of the Lord not to go to the meeting, but to remain at home and spend the evening in prayer. That night ten souls were saved!

The most interesting case, perhaps, was that of a young man who was deeply convicted when we visited the church a month or two before. He had been troubled ever since and was longing for us to return. He was one of the first to step out one night and he found Christ as his Savior. On the last night he testified splendidly and said he felt now as if his body was full of fire! Two Christian girls working in a neighboring town had felt they ought to pray every day together in the lunch hour for the other girls with whom they worked. Hearing of this campaign, they got some of them to come, and all the five who came were brought to Christ. The last night saw no open decisions, but at the very last moment when nearly everybody had gone home, the Lord saved a young man in a lovely way. I saw him standing with a group of people arguing. When I got him by himself, he said that he felt that there was something missing in his life. When I asked him if he was seeking, he answered, "I most certainly am. Only the other day I put in my diary that I was expecting something to turn up, though I was not sure what." When he saw that it was Christ that he was lacking, he very simply received Him and joined his sister, who had been converted earlier in the campaign. The thing that had caused him to come to the meeting was the evident change in his sister. And so closed a very blessed campaign.

As I look over the reports of some meetings, I blush to think that I acted sometimes with such lack of grace and wisdom. But unaware how it might appear to others, I wrote it all down.

> *March 14th to 15th 1937, Hereford.* On the Sunday afternoon I spoke to the Y. M. C. A., where we felt the presence of the Lord, and in the evening to a Methodist Church. Conscious of the spiritual deadness of the place, I put my foot on the accelerator and told them just what I thought of their bazaars, their cold respectability, their unconverted members and anything else I could think of! Some of the older members got a bit red in the face and the organist apparently was furious, for as I was giving the invitation for seekers to come to the Communion rail, he interrupted between the verses and I could say no more. Hallelujah anyway! Out of the debris, however, we gathered two or three souls for the Lord.

I did not confine myself to the Midlands, but responded to calls from other parts as they came. In 1937 I paid the first of many visits to South Wales, where the embers of the 1904 revival still smoldered.

> *6th to 15th 1937, Carmarthen, South Wales.* This was a truly wonderful time and one of the mightiest campaigns I have ever taken part in. I had the joy of having as coworker, Mr. Idris Davis, a Welsh schoolmaster evangelist who is being much used of God in South Wales. As this

was an area in which many people spoke Welsh, the
intention was that he should preach in Welsh certain
nights, while I preached in English on other nights. In the
event he preached more in English than in Welsh, because those that did not speak Welsh could not be disappointed in not understanding what he said. The feature of
the campaign was the unusual wave of conviction of sin
that came over the town. A deep solemnity seemed to
cover the place. Jokes or levity in the conduct of the
meetings seemed entirely out of place. They had not
come to be amused! By the end of the campaign, it would
be no exaggeration to say that the whole town was stirred.
Salvation was the topic of conversation everywhere, it
seemed. Some Christian bus drivers from another town,
having to stop at Carmarthen, went into a cafe, only to
find the place buzzing with talk about salvation and the
campaign. By the end there seemed to be people
everywhere under conviction, in shops and on the
streets. Nearly eighty souls made public confession of
Christ, but there were many, many more wounded birds,
who had not been brought in when I left. It was quite
heart-breaking leaving so many who needed, it seemed,
but a further word to point them to the Crucified. However, the Lord is continuing the work and His purposes
do not finish with the closing of a campaign. My last
moments in Carmarthen were spent praying with a
theological student in a garage!

It would be a long story to tell of the mosaic of the
Lord's leading that led up to the campaign, but it was
certainly one of those cases where man did not have to
raise a finger and where God unfolded His plan. A great
spirit of prayer rested on a number of the dear Christians
there and tears were often shed for the lost. Wales knows
how to weep! If we English folk wept more, more souls
perhaps would be saved. In the inquiry room, too, many
tears were shed by grown folk and young people—born
not of emotion, but of Holy Ghost conviction—and the
Savior stooped in loving compassion and lifted up many a
repentant one. The whole campaign came to a glorious
climax in the cinema service on the last Sunday night,
when we had the place packed with about 1,100.

Many stories could be told of individual cases. A bank
clerk was saved on the first Sunday afternoon and before
the week was out had testified brightly in the office and

had led his girlfriend to the Lord. One of the workers had the joy of leading his wife to the Lord at about 12 one night. He continued praying for three girls in his church until 1:30 A.M. and then went to work at 3 A.M. As we were going to the early morning prayer meeting, we met three unknown girls who were going to the prayer meeting too. They were the three girls that the Christian had been praying for up to 1:30 that morning. My hostess had been led to bring with her just three decision cards—we did not normally expect to have occasion to use them at the prayer meeting, but that day they were used and all three were saved. When we got back to breakfast, my host, who was not well enough to come to the prayer meeting, told us to our delight that he had had such a burden of prayer that he had to get down and pray for us, feeling that something was going to happen. Hallelujah, God is!

The converts testified boldly of their newfound Savior. One of the workers arriving at his place of business one morning found that a young man saved the night before had already testified, and it was before 9 A.M the talk of the place. A theological student, impressed with the new-found joy of this convert, came himself on the last night to hear and he, too, was saved. A middle-aged woman came to the women's meeting, telling her friend that nothing in the world would cause her to make a fool of herself by getting up publicly and going into an inquiry room, and yet she was the first to do so. It was moving to hear a day or two later her elderly husband calling on the Lord for mercy in his sitting room. Another night I knelt beside a poor fellow who had been in prison many times. After praying quite simply, he said, "I feel quite different already!" And as he was pointed to the promise, he said, "That's better than a Derby winner!"

A conversion which proved later to be of special significance in the campaign was that of a youth of seventeen. I could not know then all that was going to spring from that event, and therefore there was no mention of it in my report, written so soon after the campaign.

Glynn Owen had just joined the staff of the local newspaper. His immediate senior on the newspaper was an earnest Christian; and when the campaign opened, he sent this beginner to report it, his purpose being that he might have the opportunity to hear the gospel. That night Idris Davies was giving the message, and the Word of God reached the heart of that young reporter. At the end of the evening he was on his knees in the inquiry room, coming to the cross of Christ for salvation. He seemed filled with the Holy Spirit from the very beginning and immediately became an enthusiastic and compelling witness for Christ. He then went to college to study for the Presbyterian ministry, later held pastorates in North Wales and Belfast, and later still succeeded Dr. Martyn Lloyd-Jones at the famed Westminster Chapel, London.

It was not easy for Glynn Owen to fill the pulpit in the shadow of the great Dr. Martyn. But when I went to hear him there one night, he gave such a winsome and powerful presentation of God's good news for sinners, that at the end, when I tried to comment to someone on what we had heard, all I could do was to choke and stand weeping in the aisle. I went into the vestry, hugged him and said, "Glynn, go on preaching like that and I'll back you through thick and thin!" It proved, however, a difficult time for him there. Later God called him to a much larger opportunity, as minister of the Knox Presbyterian Church, Toronto, one of the great evangelical centers in North America. I visited him in Toronto myself; and as he showed me around and told me of the work, I realized how great was the task to which the one-time boy reporter, converted on his first assignment, had been called.

From Carmarthen I went to Penrheol Gospel Hall in the little town of Gorseinon, outside Swansea. This visit was to have a significance I could not have imagined at the time. This area was redolent with memories of the Welsh Revival, because it was around here that the Lord first began to pour out His Spirit in 1904. Evan Roberts was brought up at Loughor, just across the estuary. It was there that he prayed the prayer, "Lord, bend me," after listening to Seth Joshua preach—a prayer that marked a new stage in his relationship to God and that could be said to be the watershed of the revival.

My host and hostess, now in their later years, were some of Evan Roberts's first converts, and they became some of his most loyal co-workers in the revival. They would regale me with stories of the revival for hours on end until the tears ran down their cheeks. Penrheol Gospel Hall, of which they were leading members, itself came into being as a result of the revival.

As happened in a number of places in South Wales, the young converts of the revival were virtually turned out— perhaps we should say frozen out—from some of the chapels and had to start like this one. Here the embers of the revival were still smoldering, but they were only the embers. The older people, original sons of the revival, had certainly maintained the spiritual glow undiminished and were deep in the Word, but their own children, now in their late teens and early twenties, had hardened themselves against the God of their parents and attended the services only on sufferance, breaking their parents' hearts. I was hardly aware of this situation when I began the weekend of services there and did not then understand all that God did on that one Sunday evening, and how it appeared to the people. The "break," long awaited and much prayed for, had come at last. Here is the report.

20th /21st February 1937, Penrheol Gospel Hall, Gorseinon. A real breakthrough in this place. . . . It will be a long time before I forget the Sunday night meeting. As the meeting bowed in prayer after the message, just one hand was raised as a sign that the one who raised it wanted to be prayed for that he might be saved. A Welshman led in prayer, and as he was praying with all the fervor of his heart, someone was heard to be weeping and praying at the same time. No one took any notice or went to what I thought was a convicted soul. But afterward I learned she was a Christian girl who was weeping and praying for her unconverted parents. That incident seemed to bring the power of the Spirit into that meeting. I proceeded to give the invitation that the one who had asked for prayer and any others in similar condition should come forward to the front, and some ten or eleven did so. The chairman had suggested a hymn that we should sing during the invitation. Although it was unfamiliar to me, I complied, but nobody sang it; I assumed they did not know it any more than I did. I found out afterward that it was the most popular hymn in that hall, but that the Christians could not sing it because they were choked with joy and tears at seeing what was happening before their eyes. These were the very people for whose conversion to God they had prayed for so long and over whom they had shed so many

tears; and now He was at last granting them the desires of
their hearts.

The scene afterward, when each of the converts was
called upon to testify, was a scene of tremendous joy.
There were five saved in one family, a mother and four
sons. I shall not forget the face of the husband as he stood
to thank God for such a victory. Late that night, one of the
converts, a young married man, was heard singing at the
bottom of his garden, "Oh the love that sought me. . . ."
One of the girls converted that night was looked upon as
the hardest case they had had for a long time. She was
worldly to a degree. All the pleadings of Christian parents
and friends seemed only to confirm her course. She loved
the world too much ever to give it up, she said. That
night, to the joy and surprise of everyone, she was found
weeping among the seekers.

Even more was to follow at Gorseinon. There was one young
man, part of that same group of rebellious young people, who
was not present that night and who therefore missed the blessing that came to the others. His turn was to come later, when I
returned for meetings nine months after. His name was David
Shepherd, in later years to become one of the sweetest
preachers of the gospel of grace in Britain and one of her most
fruitful evangelists. But at that time he had, like the others in
his group, steeled himself against God. Like the others he had
parents who were the products of the revival and who prayed
earnestly for him. As his mother lay dying, she had pleaded
with him, "David, meet me in heaven," but he had hardened
his heart yet more.

On the Sunday of this series of meetings David sat at the
back and was careful to slip out during the last hymn before
anybody could speak to him. But he lived next door to where I
was staying, and I caught sight of him from time to time.

One day David and a friend were tinkering about with a
motor bike outside his home and I sought to engage them in
conversation about spiritual things. I was answered only with
monosyllables and grunts as they continued to work on the
machine. Eventually I said, "We cannot talk out here, fellows;
why don't we go inside?" and we went into the living room of
David's house. As I got no more response to the conversation
inside than I had outside, I said, "Do you two mind if I pray for

you?" No, they said, they didn't mind. "All right," I said, "let's get on our knees." When I had finished, David took a packet of cigarettes from his pocket and threw them into the fire, and then he began to pray and gave himself to the Lord Jesus. The other young man never opened his mouth and later, I heard, went far from God. But David was born of God before my eyes. Later he told me how narrowly God had saved him from disaster; that very night he had planned to do things for which he would have been ever after ashamed.

From that first dawning of a new life David seemed to have an unusual understanding of the doctrines of grace and the ways of God. He had heard so much for so long and had been so deeply under conviction of sin that when at last he did give in to God, it all came to life. Thereafter the first thing he did when he returned each evening from the steel works where he worked was to go into his room to spend hours over the Word of God. Later he went to the Bible Training Institute, Glasgow, for Bible training, though it is doubtful if he learned any more of the Lord and His Word than the Holy Spirit was already teaching him. But he doubtless had his experience of life broadened and gained experience in Christian service. Later, to my joy, God called him to the evangelistic staff of the very movement in which I was serving, the National Young Life Campaign, and for years we were beloved colleagues.

There is no man for whose gospel message I had, and still have, greater regard than David's; it was sweet, yet penetrating and gently intense. When it came to calling men to decision, his touch upon a meeting was light and yet the response from the people ready—an evangelist par excellence. Place after place was deeply stirred with something not unlike that revival from which his family had come, especially as he toured his native Wales. He has won great numbers to the Lord all over Britain, far, far more than I have even won. After serving the Lord with the National Young Life Campaign, he served for some years under the Movement for World Evangelization, and now he works in an independent capacity in his own land of Wales, preaching in Welsh and English.

Before we leave Wales, there is among my records the story of a campaign that gives an idea of the opposition often involved in this stern battle for souls.

3rd to 19th April 1937, Park Baptist Church, Merthyr Tydfil. It is with mixed feelings that I report this campaign. Quite frankly, the dirty old devil got in, and that through one or two Christians and chapel members! How I hate that old serpent! It was supposed to be a united campaign of most of the churches in Merthyr, and the meetings should have been big. But for various reasons the numbers right from the start were disappointing. However, the Lord did a work and some forty souls sought Christ, but there was very little impact made on this needy and sad town. The unemployment and poverty had thoroughly lowered the spirit and morale of the people, and there were great crowds of idle young men and women. Merthyr needed a great tidal wave of salvation.

For the first week I was conducting the campaign alone, and then for the last week Ian Thomas joined me. It was a joy to work with him. Our messages were directed mainly to those professing Christians inside the chapels who had not yet experienced the new birth, and there were many such. Quite a number of young people in that position, who had been baptized and made members of the chapel, came out during the campaign to receive Christ publicly, much to the annoyance of some of the chapel members! I guess the devil wasn't pleased either! One young fellow who confessed Christ the first Sunday was given such a bad time by his parents and by others who were chapel members, that he was stampeded into writing me a letter which was tantamount to recanting his action in publicly confessing Christ. Another night, after a message on "Friend, how camest thou in hither not having a wedding garment?" about eight young people came forward to receive Christ as their Savior, all of them baptized as adults.

There was such fury in the camp that night that the converts were waylaid as they came out of the inquiry room and bullied and asked what they meant by it and told there was no need for them to come out. But the converts stood firm, though some of the girls were reduced to tears. I was told afterward that if only I had asked them to come out for "reconsecration," that would not have offended anybody and there would have been a much larger response. Blow reconsecration! It is the new birth that souls need! And anyway, the Bible knows nothing of *re*consecration. If consecration is thorough and complete, it need not be repeated. *"Re*consecration" is the language of piecemeal surrender to the Lord Jesus Christ!

We had two good open air meetings in which we united with the Salvation Army, and souls were led to Christ. It was good to hear some of the converts testify after only a few days of salvation. On the last Sunday we took the local cinema on our own responsibility, much against the desires of the aforementioned chapel members. Strange how some folk have no objection to watching on weeknights the usual doubtful stuff that is put on the screen, but suddenly become pious when it is proposed to preach the gospel there on Sunday! I would preach the gospel in hell, if I could stand the heat! The best meeting of the campaign was the last one, when Ian Thomas and myself went quite mad and sang together all sorts of Negro spirituals and the like! A beautiful free atmosphere prevailed, and we rejoiced to see some eleventh-hour conversions. So hallelujah, anyway!

In the midst of this joyous battle for souls, on March 26, 1938, I married Revel Williams, the Welsh girl on the NYLC team, the student from Birmingham University. God was to give us twenty-nine happy years together.

I went through the usual throes in coming to this momentous decision. I had thoroughly enjoyed my bachelor days, packed as they were with happy service for the Lord. But as I drew near to thirty I found myself noticing that nearly every car that passed me contained two people, whereas mine contained only one. I used to think how nice it would be to have Miss Right sitting beside me! But, to use the words of the Epistle of James, I had not because I asked not; and so I began to pray. As I sought the Lord on this matter, certain criteria formed in my mind by which I felt I would recognize Miss Right—call it a check list, if you like. First, she would have to be wholly dedicated to the Lord; anything less was unthinkable. Second, she should come from more or less the same social stratum as myself. Whether the Lord thought me a snob or not, I made bold to ask Him for that. I felt it made it easier for two lives to be integrated if they came from the same sort of background. Third, I should be in love with her—the real thing, no half-measures. As I saw it, the fullness of life in Christ did not exclude romance! As an afterthought, I added a fourth—the girl in question must be across my path; I was far too busy preaching the gospel to court a girl at the other end of the country.

Revel Williams certainly fulfilled the first. She was out and out for Christ; she had a keen mind and was well read, all of which was included in her dedication to the Lord. Then too, we came from much the same social background. Moreover, I did not need to go far to court her; there she was, right across my path, a member of the very team that was helping me. However, it was on the third point—whether I was in love with her—that I had my doubts; as far as I could see I did not think I was. At that time I was sharing a flat in Birmingham with two other Christian young men (we called it the "Hallelujah flat") and we talked long about this matter.

They said, "Of course you're in love with her. You act differently toward her than toward anyone else on the team."

"Do I?" I replied, "I haven't noticed it."

"It is obvious to anyone who has eyes to see" was all they would say.

I remained unconvinced. But everything else seemed right: there was pure gold there, and I knew I would not be disappointed. It was just my personal feelings that I was doubtful of.

Eventually it came to me that perhaps I should do the same as I had done when I got saved—act in faith. After all, I reasoned, no one can guide a stationary boat, and if I began to move in this direction, God could give His guidance, either confirming or restraining as He chose. And so I began an all-important letter. It had to be by letter, because the university was on vacation and she was back home in Wales. I began very cautiously—did she not think that God had brought us across one another's paths, and ought we not to allow our friendship to become a little closer? No sooner had I penned these words than it hit me—I knew without a doubt I loved her! As the letter proceeded, it got warmer and warmer; not only was there a full declaration of my love for her, but I asked her to marry me, named the date, and asked for a telegram in reply. And I got it—"Hallelujah yes."

When she returned to Birmingham, I discovered why I had had difficulties with regard to my personal feelings. She had thought that God was calling her to be a missionary, and she was quite sure that missionaries must never look smart. She began to prepare herself for this ahead of time by wearing a style of clothes and colors (perhaps I should say non-colors) she thought appropriate, but which never suited her. The family had wanted to give her other more attractive clothes, but she had consistently refused. As a result she never attracted my eye, I being the typical male I am. So the first thing I did was to buy her a new outfit—pale blue—and did she look good! The blue showed up her dark hair to perfection, which the somber colors had never done. I was proud to be seen with her anywhere. But I was so glad that the love God put in my heart for her in the first place was not based on the attraction of the eye.

As the years passed, she came to realize more and more how important it was for a Christian woman to dress well. She had what I would call a God-given dress sense so that she always looked attractive. Her black hair turned to a silver-white quite early in life, which in no way made her look old, but enhanced her looks and gave her a rather queenly appearance.

After a short engagement (at twenty-nine I had already done my waiting), we were wed. I had to cancel meetings in my packed diary to make time for both the wedding and a short honeymoon! She on her part had to drop out of her university course; she was not likely to need the teaching diploma in the work to which we were going together. The wedding invitations were headed, "United to Fight for Jesus," and lest anyone might think they ought to appear in morning dress and top hats, a note at the bottom of the invitation read, "No glad rags"—though the best man and I did steal off to hire outselves the usual formal wear.

The wedding took place at Selly Park Baptist Church in Birmingham and was conducted by a good friend of ours, Leslie Larwood, the minister of the church. The place was full of a rejoicing crowd consisting of the team, many Young Life Campaigners, some converts from the campaigns, and Christian friends from far and near. Roy Albarn, the best man and one of our leading team members, led the congregation in gospel choruses as they waited for the service to commence. At the reception in the schoolroom Alan Redpath delivered a gospel message on the parable of the man without the wedding garment, directed to any among us who might lack the assurance of salvation. The whole thing was conducted in the joyous spirit of the campaigns in which we were engaged.

Revel and I traveled together thereafter in the work of evangelism, she filling an important role. From the start she demonstrated special spiritual gifts which blossomed more and more with the passage of years. Above all, the Lord had united us with the same vision and given us a deep love for each other. These sustained us in the years that followed, when a little boy, Michael, appeared and Revel could not travel with me. This was costly, but it was still the years of spring to us and we went on "leaping on the mountains and skipping on the hills" in the resurrection life of Jesus. Until the Lord took her in 1967, Revel was the inspirer, adviser, and trusted colleague in all that God gave me to do.

Then came the Second World War in 1939. Though the staff of the movement, as full-time Christian workers, were relieved of military service, the ruling body of the movement thought that normal evangelistic campaigns would be quite impossible with the whole country geared for war. Accordingly we were bidden to set up, each in our areas, Forces Institutes and such like, where amenities would be provided for the young service men and where we could present the gospel to them. So it was Revel and I with baby Michael moved our home from Birmingham to Beeston, Nottingham, and set up a Forces Institute there. However, after a time I discovered that evangelistic campaigns were still possible, and calls for them began to come again. I therefore left the conduct of the Forces Institute to another and returned to this work.

We found that the war, instead of curtailing such opportunities, had actually presented us with larger ones. There were thousands of young men in uniform, uprooted from home, with little to do in the evenings and with ominous prospects ahead; they presented a "sitting target" indeed for the gospel. In any case, the civilian population was still there, though subject to new pressures, and many churches were more active than ever. Right through the war and beyond, I conducted campaign after campaign in churches, town halls, and tents, even though at one place the local town council, when they saw the large white tent we had erected, insisted that it be camouflaged lest it receive unwelcome attention from enemy bombers. That meant my clambering all over its roof with a stirrup pump, spraying everything with brown paint!

In nearly every place God broke through in power, and a harvest of souls was reaped for the Lord Jesus Christ. I pick out, almost at random, a report of just one of the campaigns of those days, that at Mansfield in June 1945 as the war was nearing its end.

> The recent tent campaign in Mansfield deserves a special report in that, for the first time, the whole evangelistic staff of the movement functioned as one team in a campaign. There were four of us—David Sheppard, Calud Trigger, Jack Ward, with Roy Hession as leader. We called ourselves the Victory Team, and in humble dependence upon the Victor, we had victory all the way through. The fellowship in the team was blessing enough to our souls, but God gave us much more than this.
>
> From the very start God was with us, and the first meeting was filled with power. Numbers increased steadily, more seats had to be brought in, and toward the end the tent was packed with between five hundred and six hundred people. Souls were saved, lives made new, and homes changed—scores of them, we believe. Hardly a meeting passed without things happening like that.
>
> There were a lot of backsliders in Mansfield, but a good few of them have become frontstriders again. A number of keen Christians got filled with the Spirit—we can be keen but carnal, you know! The Mansfield Market Square offers a great opportunity for open-air meetings, and it is always possible to get a good crowd there almost any time—and we took good advantage of it even in the afternoons. We also had open-air meetings at 10 P.M. on Saturdays for those coming from the public houses—we had some lively times, I can tell you! Hardly did we ever have an open-air meeting but someone was led to Christ—though sometimes the rest of the crowd were shouting at us. They thought we were Conservative agents! One of the missions there had a brass band of men and boys, and we paraded around poor old Mansfield with that band until the streets rang again.
>
> We were told that never had Mansfield been so stirred

for years and never had the Christians from the various
sects and causes shown such love and unity in the work of
the gospel. The closing meeting was a sweet witness to
believers' oneness in their common Lord. On the last
night one of us—I won't tell you who it was—was holding
forth at some length, and someone in the congregation
heard two girls behind him saying, "I wish he would stop
and let us get out." The inference was that they wanted to
get out of the tent, but that was wrong! When the appeal
was made, they were the first to go out to the front to
confess Christ. That is what they had purposely come for,
and they found it a bit much having to listen to such a long
message before they could get saved! One thing I saw
there that I have never seen in any other campaign. At the
close of the last meeting I saw a row of people weeping
and sobbing. I thought they were under conviction of sin,
but I found they were weeping because the campaign had
come to an end!

As I look back today at the diary of engagements in those days, I
am astonished how I went from campaign to campaign with
only a few days at home in between, sometimes with no such
gap at all; and I wonder if it was fair on Revel, who was at home
alone with our little boy. But it was wartime, with countless
wives left alone, and Revel took my continual absences in the
same spirit as they did, for the war I was engaged in was much
more desperate than that against Hitler.

In 1944 Jack Ward, onetime pianist on the variety stage, was
appointed to the staff of the National Young Life Campaign,
especially to assist me. Some years before he had been led to
Christ through the Cliff College trekkers—Cliff College is a
splendid Methodist institution, founded in revival days for the
training of evangelists. After a year or two training there, he
was just beginning his own evangelistic work when I grabbed
him for NYLC. I had always made much of the singing of
choruses and gospel songs, but Jack had magic in his fingers.
With him on the piano, the singing took on a new dimension
and had a great drawing power, especially for young people.
Sometimes as I was leading the choruses, everything was so
meaningful and the congregation so wrapped up in the joys of
salvation, that I felt like taking off for glory. For the next two
and a half years Jack and I did campaign after campaign in a

happy partnership, he doubling up as pianist in the meetings and as children's evangelist earlier in the day. He has now become known to a wide circle of the Christian public in Britain by his very individual recordings of gospel music. He has since entered the Church of England ministry and is now vicar of the village of Mow Cop in Cheshire.

The climax of those years of spring came in the beautiful city of Edinburgh in March 1946. Through the initiative of a handful of zealots, local members of NYLC, a campaign was set up under the title, "Calling Youth." This gained the support of almost all the evangelical churches and made a deep impression in the city. For seventeen days the historic Assembly Hall of the Church of Scotland was crowded with intelligent young people, and from the very first they began to respond to Jesus Christ. Fifteen minutes in each meeting were given over to "Chorus Time," when I led those young people in singing, and they sang as they had never sung before, Jack's rhythmic playing ringing across the hall. By the time it came for the message they were—dare I say it?—"eating out of my hand" and the more ready for the solemn, searching message I brought.

Hundreds found new life in Christ. In my short experience I had never seen anything like it. Sometimes they were asked to walk down the aisles publicly into the prayer room; more often, interested ones were asked simply to remain in their seats for a short instruction talk, and a good company used to do so. Then having explained carefully the way of salvation and how to respond to Christ, and having given the people quiet moments in prayer to do so, I used to ask those who had taken the step to approach me as the meeting was breaking up and receive a decision booklet. And although we had counselors standing by, to whom I always passed each one on, it was found again and again that the converts needed little or no counseling. They had passed from death into life, sitting on their seats, and knew it.

This finding of peace and assurance on the part of converts without much counseling was not an uncommon occurrence in the campaigns of those years. Perhaps it has something to do with the faith of the evangelist. If he believes that seekers will need long and detailed counseling, then they seem actually to need it and do not get through to peace without it. If, on the other hand, the evangelist believes that souls receive the gift by faith even as they listen, through what Paul calls the "hearing of faith," then it is the more often found that they do thus find it. There is, of course, always the need for them to "confess with the mouth Jesus as Lord" to complete the transaction— but much seems to depend on the faith of the evangelist. My own faith in this matter has varied from time to time, I must confess; in those days it seemed stronger and more expectant than it is sometimes today.

Eight

Faith Is the Victory

ALTHOUGH THESE CAMPAIGNS were not especially large or noteworthy compared with the work of others since then—I was no big-time evangelist—their significance to me, if to no one else, was that they all sprang out of a confident application of that truth God had shown me in 1934: in His sight I had been crucified with Christ, ended not mended, and Christ was my life. Although God was shortly to deal with me much more deeply and the "bottom was to fall out" to a degree it had not before, what I was experiencing then was and is of eternal validity and can have deep significance for others.

To apply the truth of "Not I, but Christ" in practice does not mean mere passivity, though such texts as "he that hath entered into His rest hath ceased from his own works as God did from His" might at first suggest this. Although grace is God working for man rather than man working for God, and although we must come into an end of the latter to experience the former, there must be a right and proper cooperation on our part with that grace of God. Cooperation, mark you, not origination; the origination is wholly His, and we must see where we have taken His place and abdicate. But we must then cooperate with Jesus, the great Originator, and there is nothing passive about that. The cooperation needed from us is not merely that of a full surrender, nor only a continual availability to Him, both of which are essential, but above all, faith—

especially the faith that accepts that Christ is our life and that therefore His victory over all His foes is ours, and thanks Him for it. This sort of faith is described in the hymn by Charles Wesley,

> Faith, mighty faith the promise sees,
> And looks to that alone;
> Laughs at impossibilities
> And cries, "It shall be done!"

Indeed, when faith is involved in the battle for souls, it must go further and cry, not only "It shall be done," but "it *is* done." The victory over Satan, the great enemy of souls, has already been accomplished by the Lord Jesus Christ at His cross and empty tomb, and we are to accept and stand by faith on His.

> Great victory o'er sin and death and woe,
> That needs no second fight and leaves no second foe.

It was this sort of faith that I and those associated with me made so much of as we battled for souls, and which lay at the heart of the copious harvest of those days. Faith was to us "the victory that overcame the world" (1 John 5:4).

I did not always find such faith easy to come by in the thick of the fight. When Satan attacked me, he invariably did so on the faith-front. He sometimes overwhelmed me with a sense of the difficulties, the hardness of people's hearts, and the unlikelihood that any would be saved in the campaign. As evidence he would point to my inadequacies and my lack of suitable feelings and much else, and when I thought of all that people were expecting of that campaign, I would sometimes die a thousand deaths. True, I knew the victory was by faith, but I felt as if I was at one end of the promise and the devil at the other, tugging it away from me. Is this what is meant by Paul's word, "Fight the good fight of faith"? It was certainly my experience often.

Ideally, I should always have been riding the crest of faith and "resting in my Savior as my All in All"—what else could "leaping on the mountains and skipping on the hills" mean, to change the metaphor? Often this was so, but not always; and I needed Jesus to meet me anew and bring me into that abundant life again; and that is just what He did for me in place after place.

Every form of Christian service has its own special tests, but the test of faith I have described is especially that of the preacher of the gospel, who is given "thirty minutes to raise the dead" (as the title of one of D. R. Davies's books puts it), especially when he goes to a distant place for an extended campaign for which special preparations have been made. I used to think there was no one so "put on the spot" as the evangelist. The pastor, the Bible teacher, and even the conference speaker can give their talks and get away with it if nothing happens. Too often the people are not expecting anything to happen—and are not disappointed. Not so the one who comes to take special evangelistic services. Everything has been set up to this one end, many have been praying, and the counselors stand ready. It is easy to see how Satan can take advantage of this and seek to thrash the evangelist. Of course, the evangelist knows with his head it is going to be Jesus who will raise the dead, not himself; but he is human and goes through the same battle that Abraham did who "considered his own body now dead, and the deadness of Sarah's womb" and at first staggered at the promise of God through unbelief.

Surely this preparation and expectancy, rightly understood, should be the very thing that encourages him, for it gives him advantages denied to others. How hard it is for a pastor who has to minister continually to a people who are not praying and never expect God to work; in that case he has his own fight of faith, as much as the evangelist. For the evangelist or the pastor, faith is the only victory that overcomes the world.

For myself I can say that Jesus again and again came walking on the waters to His troubled servant "toiling in rowing" and brought him into rest. That was always the point at which the campaign took a new turn. Nearly every campaign seemed to be a spiritual crisis for me, when I entered afresh into that full salvation that I had already known, but without which there would have been nothing in that campaign.

I can remember even at this distance some of the occasions when He thus came to me and the means He used to set my spirit free. In one of my earliest campaigns I remember how burdened I was when little seemed to be happening and I felt completely inadequate. As I wrestled in prayer, Jesus came to me through the words of a hymn.

> Yes, I rest in Thee, Beloved,
> Know what wealth of grace is Thine,
> Know Thy certainty of promise
> And have made it mine.

I saw it all, "the wealth of grace" and "the certainty of promise," and that morning I made it mine. What more could I ask? That night God moved, and salvation flowed all over the place.

Another instance was when I went to the City of Nottingham a few days before the campaign to make certain arrangements, to supervise the erection of the tent and, hopefully, to prepare myself for the time ahead. That last was the one thing I never succeeded in doing, for as the day approached, that campaign loomed ever larger over me, and I found no way in which I could prepare myself for such an undertaking. I seemed paralyzed and incapable of the "big pray" I had hoped to have. Then He came to me in my need, strangely once again, through the words of a hymn.

> I seek no more to alter things or mend,
> Before the coming of so great a Friend,
> All were at best unseemingly; and 'twere ill
> Above all else to keep Thee waiting still.

I almost wept as I saw I did not need to alter or mend anything before His coming to me. He was enough for me just as I was that day, and so He proved to be in the campaign that followed. Twice in those three weeks we had to pull the tent down to add an extra section to accommodate the growing congregation; people turned to the Lord, young and old, in great numbers, and that spot on Nottingham Forest became hallowed ground for many.

A Christian man once said to me, "It is strange in campaigns that there is invariably one day above all the previous days when the break comes, after which God is seen to be at work." I know which day that is: it is the day when God brings the evangelist into a new rest, when by faith he obtains the promises. Thereafter he can say, "My Father works and I work."

Whether such travail in prayer and conflict with despair is always a prelude to victory, I do not know. One could quote the text, "If it be of grace, it is no more of works; otherwise grace is no more grace," and apply it in this way: "If it be of grace, then it is no more of struggling in prayer; otherwise grace is no more grace." But being the weak, doubting people we are, we often have to find our way to the simplicity of faith through such struggles and travail. And so it is right to say,

> Wherever you ripe fields behold
> Waving to God their sheaves of gold,
> Be sure some corn of wheat has died,
> Some soul has there been crucified,
> Someone has wrestled, wept and prayed
> And fought hell's legions undismayed.

However, I can testify that after I have done all my wrestling, weeping, and praying, victory has always been ultimately by faith, and presumably I could have got there without my painful struggles. And when I have looked on any fruit at all, I have had to write over it not "By the price I paid," but rather, "By the price I didn't pay."

As our faith grew bolder, we sometimes attempted things chiefly to demonstrate that God is and that He is the rewarder of those that diligently seek Him and to show the authenticity of the way of faith. This was very much so in the Men's Camp at Saundersfoot, South Wales, in 1937 and 1938. The NYLC permitted me to run a Holiday Camp just for men, while the rest of the staff ran the large mixed Holiday Conference in one of the university hostels in Aberystwyth, North Wales. The camp was open for four weeks, and parties came down each week to stay under canvas for varying periods. In all we touched over eighty men, most of them Christians. Being a bachelor at that time, I felt there was something rather special in getting Christian fellows together on their own sometimes. We ran it only for two years, after which I myself got married. So the bachelor club closed down with the capitulation of its leader! But in those two years it proved a unique blessing, especially the open-air meetings we conducted on the sea front of that resort, where we all learned new lessons as to the power of faith in the battle for souls. I quote from my report at the time:

> I suppose that the most outstanding thing about camp
> was the open-air meetings. Most weeks we conducted at
> least two open-air meetings, on Sundays in Saundersfoot

and on Wednesdays in Tenby. Though this meant cancel-
ing our own meetings on those days in camp, it proved a
greater blessing actually to see the Lord saving souls than
all the talking in the world about soulwinning and revival.
In camp we spoke much of the power of the risen Lord.
We said again and again that, where faith was active,
God's people would experience the working of the Holy
Spirit and see the salvation of souls; that the already-
accomplished victory of Calvary and the extent of the
willingness of God's heart was such that none could ask
or expect too much. The open-air meetings were undertaken to demonstrate this fact. We wanted God to shatter
our unbelief! We wanted to go back with a new expectancy of what God was willing to do through us. We got to
prayer and flattened ourselves out before the Lord. We
unitedly took hold of His declared willingness to save,
claimed the victory, and went out in full expectancy.

I suppose it is safe to say that none of us had ever seen
open-air meetings like them. I certainly never had! In
nearly every one of the eleven meetings we conducted
during the month of August, we saw souls coming before
the crowd to decide for Christ. As our faith got bolder, we
took more daring measures to secure the repentance of
sinners. Previously we had asked them to come to the ring
to accept a booklet as token of their willingness to accept
Christ. But then the Lord led us to ask them to kneel at
the front, on the grass or side walk, while we knelt with
them and led them to Jesus. The response was greater
than ever. Soldiers, schoolboys, middle-aged men and
women and young people were found kneeling in the
dusk of a summer evening, and on some occasions we
scarcely had enough campers to deal with all the seekers.
It was blessed in the extreme! As the meetings broke up,
the crowd would push forward to the front to look in
solemn silence at the seekers being prayed with and go
away greatly wondering.

I verily believe that the reason why God so signally
owned those open-air meetings was because they were
undertaken, not with the first idea of winning souls, but to
demonstrate to Christians the power and willingness of
God to save and to show the extent to which victory can be
claimed by faith. And we do know that unbelief was
shattered in many of the campers' hearts, and God alone
knows the effect it will have on the Christian work to

which they have gone back. One can see the same principle, but on a much bigger scale, in the life of George Muller. The work he did was undertaken not first of all because of solicitude for orphans, but to demonstrate to Christians that God heard prayer. It was for God's name's sake that it was undertaken, and therefore God worked. It was the same with Elijah on Mount Carmel. He was not very interested in fire as such, but it was in order to demonstrate that Jehovah was God that he prayed for fire from heaven; and therefore God did the spectacular. Surely there is a big principle here.

While turning to that old News and Prayer Letter of 1937, my eye fell on the message with which it began. As it seems to expound in a pungent manner that aspect of things which God was making so real to us in those days, I give the closing paragraphs of it here. It is referring to the parable of the importunate friend.

No phrase has helped me so much in recent years as that seen on a calendar once—"Prayer is not conquering God's reluctance, but laying hold of His willingness." If that man in the parable could be importunate to conquer his friend's reluctance, how much more ought we to be importunate to lay hold of our God's willingness!

But while there is no reluctance in God, who has not had the experience of hearing, as if from heaven, a voice saying, "I will not rise and give thee"? Who does not know the despair that that voice begets and how all the springs of prayer dry up at the thought that He will not rise and give us? But that voice comes not from our God! Take your stand on it—it is but the subtle whisperings of Satan playing on your unbelief! He was a liar from the beginning and he is at his old tricks again! God *will* rise and give thee! Principalities and powers are seeking to keep thee from thy rightful position in the heavenly places! Break through them all, faith-warrior, until thou dost touch the throne! He *will* rise and give thee!

Let it be said again, importunate prayer is not a constant pleading as if God were in some measure reluctant—such pleading will land you further from your desired haven than you were before—but it is faith breaking through the He-will-not-rise-and-give-thee of unbelief, cleaving a path through the armies of fears, doubts, and self-reproach, smiting the adversary by the merit of the cross in the hinder parts (Ps. 78:66), until with a claiming, taking, praising, laughing faith we receive what we have prayed for! See Mark 11:24. Satan would tell you a thousand reasons why God should not rise and give you. He will quote your weakness, your inexperience, your lack of feelings, your sins, your prayerlessness. He will point out how others tried and made a mess of things! He will point to the accumulated pile of unanswered prayers! He will tell you there is something in you which has forfeited the smile of God! He will magnify the difficulty of the undertaking and speak of God as if he were a man!

Yes, a thousand reasons why God should not rise and give thee! But importunate faith breaks through them all! It refuses to hear any argument except that God is willing! It finds in the Word of God promises and arguments to counter every suggestion of the enemy; and fortified with a thousand further reasons why God should bless, it presses through to the throne to find its petition already granted! Faith always has had to break through something! The sick woman had to push her way through the crowd to touch the hem of His garment! The Syro-Phoenician woman broke through the dispensational barrier and touched the Lord's heart! The four men carrying the sick of the palsy broke through the roof and laid him at the Lord's feet! David's three mighty men broke through the host of the Philistines and drew water out of the well of Bethlehem! In each case the faith that broke through received what it came for!

Though much water has flowed under the bridge since I wrote those words, and though grace has had to redeem me from deeper states of need than I knew then, those truths abide and are still for us today.

Nine

The Sad Decline

I HAVE SAID that the climax of these years of spring came at Edinburgh in March 1946. In that campaign I witnessed a harvest of souls on a scale that I never had before, and it took place with an ease and absence of human pressure that made it evident it was the work in the Holy Spirit and not mine. It was the high point of my experience of the work of the gospel.

Alas, I was never to touch that experience again. Instead, a sad decline began some months after. I found myself shorn of the power of the Holy Spirit, of which I had known so much previously; and yet I was committed to continue campaigns in place after place. The life of the Spirit did not seem to be flowing in me or through me as before, and the experience of easy fruitfulness that I had known was no more. I returned from meetings humbled and empty again and again.

I often went back in prayer to the truths that had once made all things new for me, that I was crucified with Christ and that He was living in me, that He was the Vine and I the branch and I tried to claim it all again and take my stance, as I always used to, that "faith is the victory." But all to no avail; He did not seem to respond to my faith. I therefore redoubled my efforts in prayer, trying to spend longer on my knees before each meeting. I took more time in the preparation of my messages, looking for new ones and refurbishing old ones. I adopted an ever more vehement style of preaching in order to get the message home, but it was simply trying to make up by my forcefulness for what was lacking of the Holy Spirit's gentle power, and I only gained for myself the reputation of the "spiritual tank." It was true; I bore down on congregations with all guns firing! I had gone right away from what I had previously learned, ceasing from self to rest in Christ. True, some souls came to Christ in each place, for He was gracious. But it was not as it had been; His presence was lacking, and the work became hard going for me and no longer a delight. Those who heard me for the first time were possibly impressed, and calls would still come for meetings and campaigns. But I knew something was missing, and so did Revel.

By this time Revel had been able to join me in the work again. While our son was little and she was at home, we found the constant separations hard to bear. But now he was older and the Lord had made it financially possible for us to send him to a Christian boarding school, which meant she could travel with me and share in the work during term-time at least. Inasmuch as she was spiritually dedicated, a gifted pianist, and knew how to counsel, it would obviously be a very great gain, we thought. She had been much looking forward to it, and yet after only a few months she was as defeated as I was and would gladly have remained at home. She not only had to watch her husband struggling in his own strength to get people to decide for Christ, but she knew that she herself had nothing to give. Sometimes she ardently hoped that there would be no response to the appeal, so that she would not have to counsel anyone afterward. The life of the Spirit had drained away from her, as it had from me, and what we were talking about just was not real to either of us.

The low point came for us in March 1947, exactly a year after that glorious high point in Edinburgh. It was at Margate, a seaside town on the southeast coast. The campaign had been well planned, and there was good potential in the meetings. But how tense and striving I was and how meager were the results compared with what God had done elsewhere! Revel quailed at the list of woman's meetings at which she was to speak most afternoons. She knew she was empty and cold in heart, and she would have given anything not to have had to scratch around each day for a message.

What caused this decline? Had I been asked at the time, I would have said that I did not know. Indeed, I am not sure that I would have been honest enough to have admitted a decline at all; or being the blind extrovert I was, I was perhaps unaware of it. Revel was certainly more acutely aware of it in herself than I was in myself. I was so busy struggling that I never stood back to assess where I was.

Later I was to see and confess both the decline and the things that had caused it. First, I had become mechanical in the work I was doing. Calls were coming from various quarters for campaigns and meetings, and without waiting to inquire the links that had given rise to those calls or the vision of those who sent them, I mechanically accepted them all, and it became a matter of gratification to me that my diary was full for a year ahead. For instance, 1946 was the year I conducted no less than fifteen full-length campaigns as well as much else, knowing little of each place and without any vision for it beforehand.

Then too, I had come into a strange bondage with regard to my messages. Because in the past the Holy Spirit had granted power to them, I came to think that they must always be powerful and I was forever looking for strong ones. I would often reject a theme as I prepared, because I feared it would not be powerful enough, not recognizing that His strength is made perfect in weakness and that sometimes we must be willing to be weak that He might be strong. It can be readily understood what striving and tension the feeling that I must always be powerful brought into my life, and this obstructed the work of the Holy Spirit.

However, by far the greatest cause of my experience in the wilderness was that I was not calling sin, sin in my life, especially with regard to my reactions to my dear partner, Revel. These reactions came about usually in this way. Up till then, as previously mentioned, nearly every campaign had proved a spiritual crisis for me, when after much wrestling in prayer and battling with unbelief, the Lord brought me through to rest in Himself. Because that process invariably ended in great victory in the campaign, I came to feel that this way of travail leading to faith must be the way. This was no problem when I was on my own; I could go to my bedroom or the "front room" as it is called in English homes, shut the door and spend as long as I liked in my personal Gethsemane. It mattered not how tense I might feel; it was just between me and God, and He could bring me into faith. But when Revel and I began to travel together and live in other people's homes, we so often felt on top of one another and I could not get alone to go through the extended process I thought necessary. This left me tense and frustrated.

As I look back now, it is clear that I had put myself under law to my self-made process. I was quick to be irritated with Revel over the slightest interference with my preparation and often spoke sharply to her. So tense did I become when some important meeting was looming up, that she had only to make the merest suggestion and she had done the wrong thing. I was so blind that I never called it sin and I never put it right with the Lord or with her. I went out to my spiritual battle again and again with such sins unforgiven and my heart and conscience uncleansed. Little wonder that I came back baffled and beaten. Had I but heard the voice of God, He was saying to me what He said to Israel of old, "Neither will I be with you any more, except you destroy the accursed from among you." Though I knew much about the principles of victory (Rom. 6 and so on), I did not know in experience the answer when I failed to apply those principles and sin came in—the power of the blood of Jesus.

By early 1947 I was in a needy state indeed. If it is true that need and declension make a man a candidate for the grace of God and for revival, I was certainly a candidate. As March of that year drew to a close, I little knew how near that grace of God was to a poor, defeated preacher, nor how soon the Lord would begin to work again in his heart.

Ten

"Jesus Showed Himself Again"

ONE OF THE sweetest revival texts for me now is that with which John begins the last chapter of his Gospel: "After these things Jesus showed Himself again to His disciples." I call it a revival text because it contains that little word *again;* and *again* is built into the word revival, for the prefix *re* is simply the Latin for *again.* Revival, then, is simply God doing something again. Although Charles Finney is right when he says that revival always presupposes a declension, that little word *again* indicates that Jesus is not defeated by our declension, but stoops to do again that work in our hearts which has declined. And He does so by showing Himself *again* to His disciples. That is all they need; that which has died is brought to life again, the lost joy is restored, and "barrenness delights to own His fertilizing power." And He shows Himself again "after these things," the things of despair, disappointment, and frustration.

This was exactly what the Lord Jesus began to do for two discouraged people after the events of the previous chapter, though my conception of revival then was a good deal different from what I have pictured above.

The verse goes on to say, "And on this wise showed He Himself," and the narrative tells how He did so at the Sea of Tiberias. There is a different "on this wise" for everyone to whom Jesus shows Himself again, and ours was as follows.

Over the Easter weekend of 1947 I had planned a large

conference for young Christians at Matlock, a resort area in the center of England. I had arranged for the team of missionaries from East Africa, mentioned in the first chapter, to come as the speakers. They had been in the midst of revival and were in England especially to talk on the subject. It seemed ideal that they should be our speakers; I would take the first message each morning, and the remaining sessions would all be in their hands. When it came to it, Dr. Joe Church himself was not able to be with us, but they were such a team that there were no leaders or star performers. The team who came were the Rev. Lawrence Barham, later to become a bishop; Bill Butler, then only an Anglican "deacon," but later a canon in the Church of England; and Peter Guillebaud, an educationist working in Rwanda.

Revel and I had bravely put down the theme on the brochure as "Revival is here for you—now?" a theme which was to haunt us as the conference drew near—and for this reason. Shortly before, we had returned from the campaign at Margate, which had represented such a low point for us, and discovered that the plumbing in our house had frozen in the severe winter and the pipes had burst. Revel in tears said, "I do think the Lord might have looked after our home while we were away serving Him!" and in a fit of temper she kicked a kettle which happened to be on the floor, inflicting a large dent on the unoffending article! For days that kettle and its dent remained as a memorial to the incident! In a few days we were to go away to this conference on revival, at which we were to be host and hostess, and where the emphasis was to be revival—*now*. Revel prayed desperately that the Lord would revive her before she went to the conference, because she felt it would hardly be seemly for the hostess to be revived at the conference in front of everybody! But the Lord never answered that prayer and we both went just as we were in our need—she recognizing hers, but I largely unconscious of mine.

The team's message was simple, and they made no attempt to preach in the strong way to which we had become accustomed. At first Revel was disappointed and said, "You can preach better than they can." But this much they did do—they laced everything they taught with their personal testimonies, sharing their experiences of failure and weakness on the mission field and how grace had restored them—and this in the event proved inescapable to everybody.

However, the content of what they taught was very different from my own conception of revival. The first subject was the story of Cain and Abel—Cain, the man who offered the fruit of the ground (representing our own works), and Abel, who offered the firstling of his flock (representing the blood of Jesus the Lamb). This was a theme I had preached on myself, using it as an evangelistic message to the unconverted, and I could not see its relevance to revival. Later I would understand this was just what I needed, that I was indeed a Cain rather than an Abel, that I had been trying to get from God the power and blessing I needed by my own works rather than coming by to the cross of Jesus for cleansing in His blood—that is, I had been struggling instead of repenting. Little wonder that the Lord had not accepted me and my offering, when, evangelist though I was, I was in effect by-passing the cross as regards my own current needs.

Revel very quickly humbled herself and knew what it was to be restored by the blood of Jesus, and she did not care who heard her prayer of confession in the particular prayer meeting in which she responded to Him. Nevertheless, I remained high and dry—dry just because I was high. I was mainly concerned with how this simple, disconcerting message fitted in with my victorious life message; where was Romans 6, 7, and 8 in this quiet insistence on repentance and the blood of Jesus?

The team seemed more concerned about the leader of the conference than with almost anyone else, and they began to counsel me. I who had so often counseled others was myself being counseled, and it made it all the harder when my own wife joined them in their counseling, saying, "But can't you see it, Roy . . .?"

One day Bill Butler told me, "Roy, I think you need to repent."

"But where do I need to repent?" I answered. Quite honestly I just did not know, for few could be working harder for God than I was. My words were a repetition of the people's reply to Malachi, when he bade them to return to the Lord: "Wherein shall we return?"

"Frankly, I don't know," Bill said, "but I am sure you need to. Revival began for me when I repented."

We had nearly terminated the conversation when he added, "By the way, I think I could suggest where you might begin. Do you remember when we arrived at the conference and we met you for the first time? You had to go to one of the other houses to make some arrangements and you told us to jump into the car and go with you. There you gave some instructions to a young lady [it was Revel] but you did not introduce us on that first occasion and we did not know by the way you spoke to her whether she was your secretary or your wife. Perhaps you ought to begin there—I certainly had to begin by repenting with regard to my attitudes toward my wife."

When at the end of the conference others testified as to how Jesus had enabled them to repent and had filled their hearts to overflowing with the Holy Spirit, I had no such testimony. It was only afterward that I gave up trying to fit things into my doctrinal scheme and came to the Lord for cleansing from my personal sins. This did not prove the great crisis I had thought, for the Lord simply asked me to begin with the obvious—my tenseness, my consequent sharpness with Revel, my wrong reactions to this or that as they arose. I discovered that revival does not come by doing some big thing, but rather by being cleansed of little things. That is, in effect, what Naaman had to see: "My father, if the prophet had bid thee do some great thing, wouldst thou not have done it? How much rather then, when he saith to thee, wash, and be clean?" For me it was like beginning my Christian life all over again. My flesh "came again like the flesh of a little child," as did Naaman's when he was humble enough to dip himself in Jordan. To put it another way and to use the other Old Testament picture, what happened that day was that I confessed that I was nothing more than a Cain; but the moment I did so, I found myself an Abel, coming with nothing but the blood of Jesus, and accepted by God as a sinner.

Repenting of such things as my attitudes toward Revel was, however, only the beginning. I found myself involved in a trail of further repentances, for the Lord had much to show me. Sometime after, Revel said to me, "Roy, if you really want to get right with the Lord, I think you will have to get right with

. . ." and she mentioned a man on a certain committee with whom I had had a disagreement.

"Do you realize," she added, "that he has not spoken to you since then, and that was a year ago?"

I felt that only showed how wrong he was, holding a grudge for so long. But the Lord showed me I was wrong too—indeed, the first to be wrong. He was the chairman of the committee of which I was the executive secretary. The matter being discussed was a sum of money, whether it should be sent to the headquarters of the society in London or be retained locally. He had persuaded the committee to take the latter course, but I was quite convinced that the former was right and sent the money on. When he heard, he did not seem to appreciate it, to put it mildly, and the telephone wire carrying his comments became quite warm! I explained how right I was, and I thought he understood. But apparently he had been unimpressed with my arguments, and although he was my brother in Christ, he had avoided me since. When I sought the Lord, He showed me that I was not so right as I thought. Though the actual sending of the money might have been right, I had done it in the wrong way. There was another way, the way of the Lamb. It would have taken longer, and we would have needed to talk further, but ultimately we could well have come to be of one mind. In a sense it was a relief to me to see this, for now I knew where to repent. I phoned to ask if I could come and see him. He answered rather gruffly, "What do you want to see me about?"

There was nothing for it; I had to make my confession on the telephone, It was done very simply.

"Do you remember that situation?" I asked. "Brother, I was wrong, please forgive me."

Immediately love and fellowship flowed over the line. Later he invited me to speak at the church of which he was the secretary and himself took the chair, telling the people what had happened between us and how we had been reconciled.

On another occasion we were having a conference for ministers and their wives. Revel was not able to be present. The lounge was full, and I was sitting on the floor. The power of the Lord was present to heal, and people were sharing what God had been saying to them. One young minister recounted how he had been convicted of deep selfishness toward his wife; he had refused her the money for a new pair of shoes on the ground they could not afford it, and yet a short while before he had bought himself an expensive motor mower for the lawn. Somehow those words deeply touched me. A week before, I had been completing the preparation of a message I was to give at a big hall on the final night of an evangelistic campaign. I was tense and without peace in my heart, and when my wife bade me hurry up and come down to the car lest we be late, I was irritated. When we got to the hall, I was in such haste to get out of the car that I slammed the door hard behind me, crushing her fingers. They were bruised and bleeding, and she obviously could not play the piano that night. Of course, I was extremely sorry and said so, but it was the hardest night's preaching I had had for a long time. We had both dismissed it as an unfortunate accident; but a week later as that young minister told of the wrong he had done his wife, Revel's bleeding fingers came before me and the Lord showed me it was not really a mere accident. I would never have slammed that door as I did, had I not been tense and lacking in peace. Then I saw the hands of Jesus and the hurt that I had inflicted not only on Revel but on Him; and I wept like a child before them all. Just as soon as I could, I got on the telephone to her and I shared what God had shown me and begged her forgiveness.

An interesting illustration of how one person's openness about himself can help another was when I felt Revel did not know fully enough how it was between me and the Lord. There was a range of things, such as impurity of thought, which I was dealing with before the Lord and receiving cleansing for, but about which it never occurred to me to share a testimony with her. As a result she did not really know the man who sat opposite her at the breakfast table every morning, and, as it turned out, I did not really know her. Loving as our relationship was by ordinary standards, we were to some extent strangers to one another when it came to the deepest things. As I shared my experience of grace in areas she did not know, it encouraged her to reveal things I did not know about her. She confessed that she had been struggling with an inferiority complex with regard to me when it came to spiritual things. I seemed to spend, she said, so long in my study, praying and studying the Bible, that she was quite sure I would despise her simple prayers. This tied her up and made her reluctant to pray in front of me. We did, of course, pray together, but when it came to her turn to pray there was often a long pause before she was able to break through. As I shared what Jesus had to do for a sinner like me, she lost her inferiority complex; and she lost it, basically, through calling it sin and asking God's forgiveness for it. If I was willing to take the place of a sinner, she could afford to do the same, and we experienced a new oneness at the cross of Jesus, where sins are washed away. From that day she began to blossom in her spiritual life and service as never before and became one of the most helpful and able of women speakers.

At that original conference at Matlock, one of the things that touched me deeply was a motto card designed by Dr. Joe Church. It illustrated the words, "Not I, but Christ," on which the "C" of Christ was shown as a bent "I."

NOT I, BUT CHRIST

Galatians 2 20

The first time I looked on it, it pierced me to the heart, especially when I looked at the words underneath it, written by Bill Butler:

> Lord, bend that proud and stiff-necked "I,"
> Help me to bow the neck and die,
> Beholding Him on Calvary,
> Who bowed His head for me.

I saw I was the proud, stiff-necked, unyielding man pictured in the letter *I,* so quick to justify himself and to resent others.

More moving to me was to see that same man on his knees, with his head bowed and his face buried in his hands. He had seen Jesus and, ashamed, had taken the sinner's place and given up his rights to Him. I was immediately convicted that I had not been taking that place, nor had I been willing to bow the head and die to self. It was natural for me to stand up for myself. Little wonder that Jesus had not been able to live His life in and through me in all its sweetness and fullness. But I saw, too, in those days a new value in His blood which "makes the wounded whole."

It was as a direct result of Jesus' showing Himself to us again at that time that Revel and I wrote jointly the articles that became *The Calvary Road.*

Eleven

The Expanding Bridgehead

THE BLESSING THAT God gave to those who attended that conference in Matlock He gave elsewhere, wherever the team went. Although the results were never spectacular (the team were just not aiming at the spectacular in any case), individuals experienced conviction of sin, a deep brokenness at the cross of Jesus, and cups filled to overflowing. The team told no dramatic stories of what happened in East Africa which might have caused us to yearn for like things in England. They merely gave their testimonies and the simple Bible teaching on which they based everything and said in effect, "What has happened to us can happen to you right now, without your having to wait for some mighty visitation from Heaven."

As they left Uganda for Britain, Simeoni Nsibambi, the old saint and prophet of revival there who for health reasons has been confined to his house for years, said to them, "Just ask God to give you one man; and if He does so, you can return saying revival has come to England." That, then, was all they were after: one man. God gave them "one man" many times across England, people who had seen a new vision of the Lord and had entered into a new chapter in their relationship with Him. It was not long before a distinct movement of the Holy Spirit was discernible among Christian leaders and lay people, who began to relate to one another on the basis of what God had done for them. A small bridgehead of revival had been established in England, a bridgehead which continued to expand long after that original team returned to Africa. This was, and is, no exclusive group of people; wherever men are willing to bow their stiff necks at the cross of Jesus, He establishes His bridgehead in their hearts, and personal revival comes.

To those who have grown up since World War II, the term *bridgehead* may not convey a very definite picture. The establishing of a bridgehead was the military strategy used when, for instance, the allied armies invaded Italy from North Africa. Instead of invading on a broad front, the Allies selected just one spot on the coast and landed men and armaments there; in that case it was, I believe, Salerno. They then proceeded to strengthen and expand what they now called the bridgehead, landing more and more men and equipment, from which they were able at the right moment to move out and fan victoriously over the countryside.

So, revival for us in England differed from the experience of revival in some other places, in that it has not been a sudden and mighty invasion of the Holy Spirit on a broad front, but rather the establishing of a bridgehead of revival in a few hearts, and then the slow but steady expansion of that bridgehead. It has continued thus for the thirty years since those early beginnings, until today it is so extensive that no one person could possibly keep track of it; and it has come about by the continual implementation of the "one-man" vision. And who knows what other bridgeheads of grace are expanding to the blessing of His people, bridgeheads with which we may not have had personal touch.

What was the message the team from East Africa brought with them that affected so many so deeply? They actually did not bring any new message not already fundamentally acknowledged by every Bible-believing Christian. They sought to describe and share the inward nature of revival in which they had been living along with many others. This was not easy, because it was not a case of systematic theology but rather of *life*, which was flowing everywhere among tens of thousands of Africans and missionaries. Dr. Joe Church, in planning to come to England, summarized the revival under five points.

1. *Prayer with a hunger.* Revival begins with a great

dissatisfaction with the low spiritual life of the church in general and of oneself in particular. Seeing that something better is promised in the Word of God, one prays with hunger for new life to be given, beginning in oneself.

2. *Brokenness at the cross.* The process of revival is a continuous moral choice that the proud, stiff-necked "I" in every one of us should be bent and broken, and that our rights in everything should be yielded to God. Brokenness is simply the response of humility to the conviction of God, which is, of course, continuous. It is the willingness for all the humbling that real repentance and confession of sin involves. That can take place only at the cross where we see One who was made "a worm and no man" for us, and who yielded up His rights to pay the price of our sin. A hard, unyielding spirit makes revival impossible.

3. *Fullness.* Hearts filled to overflowing with the Holy Spirit—that is revival in its positive aspect. As David said, "My cup runneth over." And ours may be continuously running over with joy in Christ, love to others and praise to God and when that is so, others get the blessing. But the Lord Jesus does not fill cups dirtied by envy, bitterness, resentment, doubting, complaining, etc. Sin must all be confessed to Him that it might be cleansed in His blood.

4. *Openness.* The condition of fellowship with God and our brother and also of the cleansing of the heart is "walking in the light" (1 John 1:7), that is, openness. Real fellowship is established when we are open about ourselves and admit our faults.

5. *Oneness.* Lack of oneness between us and others is sin, and until we are prepared to deal with sin in every one of our relationships, we shall not be filled with the Spirit. Everything that comes between us and another comes between us and God. Our relationship to God is not one whit better than our relationship to our brother. Little wonder that the Holy Spirit has withdrawn Himself from us for so long in grieved silence.

Not that the team mechanically put out these points in every meeting. Indeed, when William Nagenda and Yosiya Kinuka, two of the African leaders in revival, came to join the team after a few months, they were quite innocent of the five points; they had come simply to preach Jesus as they knew Him, and yet their ministry was, if anything, more penetrating and helpful.

The team took up Scriptures and messages as the Lord led them, but this summary of revival as they saw it was the background of their thinking.

About this time the material which later became *The Calvary Road* began to be written. Revel and I had been issuing a little monthly paper called *Challenge*, intended to lead young Christians into a deeper experience of the Lord, and we were coming to the end of what we had to say. It was nutural, then, that in the following issues we should record what God had newly shown us. In the first four we simply put down the themes the team had brought to us and the telling illustrations they had used. Then in the next issues we wrote fresh messages the Lord gave us, all in the light of the new experience of Him.

There was a sudden and surprising demand for the paper because it carried this simple message. Letters came in almost every day telling us of the way God was blessing His people through it, and asking for further supplies. Requests, too, arrived from distant countries to which the paper was finding its way, as did news of the beginnings of revival in the lives of God's people in various parts. We had nothing to glory in, for it became evident that revival was not so much the result of *Challenge*, as *Challenge* was the result of revival. God was at work in many people's hearts across the world, and their testimony made others hungry; these in turn found their way to repentance and the Cross, and so the blessing spread. With it the little paper seemed to go, for it sought to express in clear and scriptural language what so many were beginning to experience.

Circumstances made it difficult for us to continue sending out further issues of *Challenge*, yet requests for back numbers kept coming. So we put together some of the more helpful numbers with extra chapters, and the Christian Literature Crusade in England published it as *The Calvary Road*. I little knew then that edition after edition would be called for in Britain and the United States, and that this would continue right on to the present, with the circulation increasing rather than decreasing with the years. Nor did we dream that it would be translated into so many languages. As I have traveled the world, I have heard incredible stories of what God has done in lives and situations through it. It has simply been caught up by the Holy Spirit in calling the church back to repentance and the power of the blood of Jesus. Yet, at the time it was simply an expression of what a small but expanding bridgehead of people were learning about a true walk with God.

When it first came out, I felt embarrassed sometimes when I rose to speak at a meeting, feeling quite sure that those who had read the book would be disappointed when they met and heard me. But such self-consciousness was needless: the book did not claim that the author had attained some special degree of holiness and humility, but rather it revealed where he had not attained and called him back to the Cross. It was essentially a book by a sinner for sinners, showing the rich provisions of God's grace.

As I look through the short articles with which I used to begin each of my News Letters, I can trace something of the progression of my thinking. There had been much about the indwelling of Christ, the fullness of the Spirit, and the faith which brings the victory—but little about repentance and brokenness; still less about the power of the blood of Christ to restore the failing saint and set him free. This was the new note that *The Calvary Road* struck.

One factor contributed more than any other to the bridgehead, and that was that the Lord brought a number of leaders together who had been newly touched by Him. As I traveled around, I heard of this person and that in whom something new had obviously happened. I heard, for instance, of a young vicar, Fred Barff, who had shared with his congregation God's recent dealings with him and had asked from the pulpit their forgiveness for his wrong attitudes toward them. It was obvious that we ought to come together and encourage one another in the new path we were following. Peter Marrow, a vicar in a London suburb, took the initiative and invited some ten of us to spend two days together in his vicarage. He opened the gathering with the words, "We've not come together to talk about revival, but to be revived."

Actually, that was exactly what I had come for—to talk about revival. But as soon as those words were uttered, I was convicted of something in my heart (I cannot remember now what) which I had to confess to the Lord on the spot, and then I was able to contribute a testimony instead of just some doctrinal point. We spent those days sharing what Jesus had been doing in our lives, hiding nothing, looking deeply into one another's hearts, and we came to know and love one another as sinners in whom Jesus was doing a new work. More than that, we discovered we had become a team—we knew that we were in something infinitely precious together, and that He was giving us a vision for revival in our country.

Were it not for that deep joining in heart, the blessing we had received would have remained only an individual matter and would largely have been dissipated with the passage of time. More than that, there would have been no sense of movement, no discernible flowing of a river. But a river of blessing did begin to flow out to others from that little group as we began to act together. First, we had to go much deeper with one another than that one gathering allowed, and we arranged other meetings. Then several of us would visit this or that church as a team. It was quite new to some congregations to see ministers setting aside their own church work to share new and costly testimony as to the things God was teaching them, and God touched others as a result.

Then we undertook various residential conferences, some for ministers and others for laymen. These proved heavenly times of breaking down and lifting up, and yet others entered in. A minister at one early conference wrote of how the Holy Spirit worked:

> It was most glorious how the Lord revealed Himself to us and drew us back again to the cross in repentance. Two of the things that He showed me were the wonder of "It is finished" all over again, and also the need of recognizing His conviction of sin. He does not seem to shout at me when He convicts. His presence in the meetings was very real as once again He stood in the midst and showed His hands and His side. I don't think I have ever seen such a breaking down as He gave us there. There were about fifty or so—vicars, ministers, and Christian workers of various sorts and kinds and ages. They were all hungry, so God met with them. A torrent of sin, some indeed almost unbelievable in the people concerned, came pouring out and was cleansed away in the precious blood of Jesus. Many went back to their parishes to face their church councils and congregations and so on, to put things right;

and some could not wait even until they got back but wrote off letters straight away.

The experience of one minister, John Collinson, was typical. Looking back after twenty-eight years, he tells what that time meant to him. The Lord was later to give him, as a result, a revival ministry right across Britain.

In spite of having been deeply blessed in Africa through meeting the leaders of the East African revival seven years earlier, it was a very dry and needy vicar and ex-missionary who arrived at the conference at Elfinsward, having told the Lord that he could not leave that place unless He did some new thing in his cold heart. I could not foresee what He would do, but it seems now that during every session He led me to the cross. I had always preached "Christ and Him crucified," but I knew little, if anything, of the cross in my own life. Now I began to see it in a very different way. I saw how Jesus had been crucified not only for my shameful sins, but for the everyday respectable sins which I swept under the carpet. It was a fresh revelation to see Him for my sake becoming on the cross "a worm and no man." It was a new thing to see Him consenting to be despised and rejected of men and put to an open shame for the sins I counted as of little importance. There on the cross He was willing to have no rights, and all this because He loved me. I saw that, unlike Jesus, I expected as a vicar to be treated with respect. I usually claimed my rights. I did not like criticism because it endangered my reputation. I seldom admitted I was wrong or said I was sorry. Beneath the cross more and more of self came into view: hard self in the home; proud self in His service; hurt self when misjudged or misunderstood; corrupt self in the secret imaginations of my heart. It shocked me to discover that all He was, I was not. Instead, self was prominent everywhere. I felt that nobody in that conference could need forgiveness and cleansing more than I, yet I could not confess the state of my heart and admit that I was the kind of person the Holy Spirit was showing me to be.

After a long and sleepless night, in the early hours of the Thursday morning, God gave me the gift of repentance. I saw that Jesus was put to an open shame, taking upon Himself in public all the sins I shrank from admitting I had committed. In the light of His exposure, how could I go on hiding and saying I was innocent? As I saw Him yielding to the sin-bearing and shame of the cross which I deserved, He melted my heart and with tears I told Him I was willing for that walk on the Calvary Road with Him. He bent my proud neck there and I admitted the truth of all He had been showing me. The burden was lifted and I knew His precious blood had cleansed. With what I now know was the Holy Spirit, my heart was filled to the brim and running over.

A few hours later, after the address at the morning meeting, came the first practical step of dying. Still fearful and unwilling to be a fool for Christ's sake, I shared in a very hesitant way what He had shown me. It was painful for me and perhaps for others present, but a great sense of relief of not having to keep up a show any more followed.

On the following Sunday at home I felt during the morning and evening services I should tell my congregation what the Lord had taught me at the conference and how at Calvary He had cleansed me afresh in His precious blood and set me free. Now the last rag of my reputation, which I valued so highly and to which I had clung for so long, was thrown away and I was sure my congregation would leave the church that night, never to return. This I knew was part of what "dying with Christ" meant. Very understandably, some disliked intensely what they heard. One said, "It was frightful. If you, our vicar, are like that, what hope is there for us?" Some others saw the cross and wept. From that Sunday God's reservoir, the channels of which had been clogged by unrecognized and unrepented sin, found new outlets. Life-giving streams, welling up from broken and contrite hearts, began to flow very quietly together, swelling the stream of new life in our district.

What began at that conference, not only revived my ministry, but changed the whole direction of my life. Praise the Lord!

Later the Lord led us to undertake together an annual conference in the summer, lasting four weeks, different parties coming each Saturday. We took over Clarendon, a girls' boarding school of great beauty in Abergele, North Wales, one of the most scenic areas of Britain. As most of the team were ministers with heavy church responsibilities, I became responsible for the organization. The ministry was not undertaken by well-known speakers called in from outside, but simply by those who had been newly touched. There was always much openness and sharing among the increasing numbers who came, and I heard testimonies of such depth and reality as I had never heard before. Wrong personal relationships and hidden sins were revealed and put right. People allowed Jesus into their home life at a deeper level, and marriage relationships were made quite new. He was allowed, too, into the life and service of many a minister with beautiful results, and church members repented of criticizing their ministers. I found myself saying, "I never saw it on this wise before; how was it that I missed things like this in my campaigns all these years?" The reason was that I was now letting the Lord work in my heart, and I was no longer the hard-hitting evangelist, but simply one of the penitents.

For twenty-five years I undertook this responsibility, first with Revel, and then when the Lord took her, with my second wife, Pam—until in 1974 John Collinson took over from me. As the numbers grew (ultimately nearly two thousand passed through the conference in the four-week period), we found it a tremendous undertaking, as we had to arrange every detail, from the cooks in the kitchen to the speakers on the platform, with registrations flooding in over the months running up to the conference. The work seemed to be with us throughout the year and had to be fitted in with our itinerations.

Sometimes during the immense labor at the beginning of a conference, Revel and I would say, "Never again; this will be the last." But when, as we progressed, we saw the blessing God was giving and the lives He was transforming, we were ready for the next one. Revel used to say, "We'll continue to run this conference just as long as the Lord sends us cooks!" Speakers were not our problem—they were a dime a dozen! But dedicated cooks—ah, that was another matter! Yet the Lord sent us cooks, and we continued to run the conference. Sometimes when I was inclined to complain of the toil and sweat of it, the Lord would show me that if I spent a whole year trekking from church to church in Britain, not as much would be achieved as through the one month of the conference.

To give an insight into the manner of the Spirit's work at these conferences, I quote as typical the experience of two men who have since become distinguished evangelical leaders in

Britain. The first is Arthur Bennett, a Canon in the Church of
England and lecturer at All Nations Christian College in
southeast England.

> As a young incumbent of a well-known evangelical
> parish I attended my first revival conference at Abergele
> in 1951. My immediate reactions were noncommittal, but
> I could not help being impressed by the sense of life
> manifested by speakers and guests. As a "traditional"
> evangelical I had gone to the conference in a spirit of
> self-sufficiency, which as the week went on began to be
> revealed as an area of deep need, especially in the spheres
> of self-centeredness, independence, and pride. I saw my
> want in the personal testimonies of fellow ministers that
> unveiled my own heart. From college days smoking had
> taken hold of me as a means of reaching men. I then saw
> how futile it was, and before the conference ended I
> burned matches and tobacco in an Abergele copse and
> threw my pipe far over the trees. That and other things
> marked a major change in my life and ministry.
>
> The following Sunday I dispensed with sermons and
> told the congregation what Jesus had done for me, and
> how that week I had learned the power of His blood as a
> present virtue to meet my needs when I continually
> repent of my sin and come in true humiliation to Him.
> After the evening service one of my leading churchmen
> said to me, "I always knew I had a vicar; I now know I have
> a brother."
>
> The effect was greatly felt in my home relationships, for
> I now saw that if Christ is not dealing with us here, there
> can be little victory elsewhere. In this sphere I found I
> must be open about myself to my wife and children, and
> be willing to take the blame in a sinner's place. The Lord
> has taught us through the years that as we have repented
> toward each other we have found a unity and a life we had
> not known before.
>
> That conference and those that followed have made my
> ministry, with all its failings, what it has been and given a
> love within the family that I would not at one time thought
> possible. Along with others I cannot thank God enough
> for teaching me the great truth that the way of victory is
> the way of brokenness by seeing Jesus and His blood.

The second is the Rev. Stanley Voke. As a result of his new
meeting with the Lord, he was later to take his place in the

growing team of men who led these conferences, as did Arthur Bennett. At the time of which he writes he was minister of the Bethesda Baptist Church, Sunderland, and has since become one of England's leading Baptist ministers.

The year was 1950. I was an energetic, proud, tense pastor of a large church in the north of England. Outwardly successful, I lived a life of inward defeat. Our marriage appeared happy enough but was full of tensions, and I was warned by my doctor of serious duodenal trouble within two years if I did not learn to live in peace.

At this time, a tea-planter fresh from revival in Uganda, William Turner-Russell by name, visited our church and in a personal conversation said to me, "You need revival in your heart. It will begin when you start to repent of your sins and see the cleansing blood of Jesus." I was offended by this, but that week the Lord began to show me one thing after another about which I needed to repent both to Him and to others in the home and the church. He did this by first convicting others who came confessing to me where their attitudes toward me had been wrong. Soon we had a sweet, repenting fellowship in the church. It was only the beginning.

At the first conference we attended at Abergele in 1951, God brought my wife, Doreen, to know for the first time the rest and joy of forgiveness. I was a "convention speaker" ready to speak, with a sheaf of special addresses. Not one of them was given! Instead the Lord searched my heart while I argued with the brethren that their messages were all too simple, that repentance was not for Christians, and so on. One night I went to bed angry about it all. I awoke at dawn when it seemed that the Lord was there showing me two pathways, one of unbrokenness, the other of brokenness and repentance, the first a lonely way ending in darkness and ruin, the second a way of fellowship leading into light. I was afraid to take this way, when Jesus seemed to reach out to me and draw me into it very gently—the way of grace. I am go glad I went with Him.

We had much to learn together after this, many breakings and repentings to one another, to the children and to others in our churches. But Jesus has been very patient with two strong people who naturally found it hard to break and say sorry. But we came to see this was "the way," and the cross was always the door into it. The gospel began to live again, the Lord became real, His blood once more was precious, and the love of the brethren sweet and deep. The way has been one of increasing light in which blessing on blessing has come in our marriage and our ministries in several churches and in various parts of the world. If we could sum up these twenty-seven years of walking with Jesus in His way of grace, it could only be in the song of two continually forgiven sinners . . .

> Glory, glory, hallelujah,
> Glory, glory to the Lamb.
> Oh, the cleansing blood has reached me,
> Glory, glory to the Lamb.

As the years passed, so many wanted to come to these annual holiday conferences from all over the country that we had to change our venue several times for larger premises. In this way the blessing has spread right across the British Isles and, as we shall see later, to other countries too. That little team that met as a group of weak men in that vicarage in 1947 is no longer little; so many have had their ebbing spiritual experience revived and are walking with a vision of revival for others, that we hardly know now where the team begins or ends.

There has been much interchange of fellowship over the years between the team on the Continent and that in England as the spirit of revival has spread.

Back in 1947 and the early 1950s all this was, of course, hidden from our eyes—we were only beginning. I must therefore tell of an outstanding event in 1950, in which four of us participated, which meant a further stage in our development and understanding of revival. This was our first visit to East Africa to link up again with the brothers who had helped us so much and to share in what was going on there. The river of revival had been flowing in East Africa without interruption for no less than twenty years, beginning in Rwanda and Uganda in 1930. By 1950 it had become a mighty "river with waters to swim in, a river that could not be passed over," flowing all over East Africa. Accordingly we went with great expectations— and we were not disappointed. Immediately on returning I wrote the report which constitutes the bulk of the next chapter as it appeared in *Floodtide*, the magazine of the Christian Literature Crusade.

Twelve

Revival in East Africa

THE DAY WAS Sunday, April 23, 1950; the time just before
sunset, after which darkness always comes quickly in the
tropics; and the place mighty Lake Victoria in Uganda. A giant
flying-boat came out of the sky to make a perfect landing on the
shimmering waters of the lake; it was part of the regular service
in those days between Great Britain and Uganda, operated by
British Overseas Airways Corporation. It brought four of us
from England to witness for ourselves the revival that was
spreading through Uganda, Kenya, Tanzania, Rwanda, and
Burundi, and to share in the blessing that God was pouring out
on both Africans and Europeans. Our little party comprised
Peter Marrow and Fred Barff—both of them vicars of Anglican
parishes in Britain—Fred's wife Constance, and me.

As we owed so much to our brethren, it was natural that
when the opportunity presented itself to renew fellowship with
them, we should grasp it with both hands and make the trip.
There was at the time an occasion that would draw together in a
special way the revival brethren in East Africa, and an invitation had been sent us. God provided the money—in a different
way for each of us—and so we came, eager to learn and
experience more deeply that which lies at the heart of revival.

The special occasion was a conference of leaders from all
these territories, which was to be held at Kako in Uganda.
There were present about 1,000 African leaders and 150 Euro-

pean missionaries. There would easily have been many times that number had it not been decided to restrict the number of African delegates from each area.

What impressed me first of all was the oneness among the Christians. Representatives of some thirty tribes, who but a few years before were continually at one another's throats, were seen embracing one another, eating together, and praising the Lord in deepest fellowship. An African king and an African prime minister, both of them saved, were as ready to testify to what Jesus had done for them and sing the African praise chorus as were the poorest in the land. Best of all, the grace of God had achieved a deep oneness and trust between European and African—no pride or superiority in the one, nor inferiority, resentment, or jealousy in the other. They were completely free with one another.

Those who knew Africa told me that normally there is bitter hatred of the European and that this is so even in the professing church, though skillfully hidden under the surface. But here in the revival, the love of Jesus had obliterated the barriers. This fellowship was not created by the European trying to live more like the African and becoming increasingly condescending. There have been those who have tried to do this. But when they have done it all, the barriers remain and oneness has not been achieved. But when all are willing for self to be revealed and confessed at the cross, fellowship is achieved immediately.

The second impression I gained was that of the tremendous paean of praise that goes up all the time to the Lord Jesus. The spirit of praise and rejoicing in Him is perhaps one of the most prominent features of the revival. Again and again the addresses would be interrupted by the African praise chorus breaking forth from hearts filled with the vision of the glory of the Lamb.

> Tukutendereza Yesu,
> Yesu Omwana gwendiga . . .

It is a chorus praising Jesus, the Lamb of God, for His blood which cleanses from sin, and it is sung everwhere there. At the close of the service, as the great crowds were filing slowly out of the Anglican church, the same chorus would continually sweep the whole company; and when they left the church, it was only to stand in a great crowd and praise and praise. I was sometimes near to tears as I watched this praise to Jesus for His atoning blood, and I thought how precious it must be to Him. Truly, here was the reward of His sufferings.

The praise would reach an even higher level whenever anyone was saved. After the first two days this began to happen, although it was a conference arranged primarily for leaders. There was never any appeal for people to raise their hands or go into an inquiry room. The Holy Spirit Himself would convict a man, and as he left the church, he would begin to testify to one or two around him that he had been saved. The news would spread quickly, and then there would be a scene of rejoicing almost impossible to describe. The first time I saw it I could hardly believe my eyes. A large crowd of Africans were singing praises with more than usual vigor and waving their arms. As I pushed forward, I saw a middle-aged man standing humbly in their midst. One after another, Africans came up to him and threw their arms around him. I learned that he was a leading member of the very church in which we had been meeting. He was a man who had long resisted the call of Jesus, but he had just given in and had found peace. Suddenly someone held up his hand and the singing was silenced while he gave his testimony in a few broken sentences. Then the praise continued with even greater joy, as did the embracings of the returned sinner. We Europeans who were near embraced him, too, and sang with the rest. What a welcome into the kingdom of God for a poor sinner! This happened to everyone who was saved, or in whom the Lord won a special victory.

It might be thought that this was merely African emotionalism and therefore superficial. Far from it! I was to realize something of the spiritual depth of these men when, on being introduced to me, one of them spoke English said, "Roy Hession? I am so glad to meet you. We have read your book *The Calvary Road* and we enjoyed it very much. We always like to meet the author of a book which has helped us, that we might know if he is broken." By brokenness I came to understand that they meant a man's willingness to take his place as a sinner on any matter God showed him. Nothing very superficial there!

That this was the supreme concern of the African revival leaders was apparent when I was asked to bring a message. I had not come to speak, simply to learn, but I found myself so adopted into the fellowship that I was expected to take my place in the team. On three occasions in my message I told personal experiences of taking my place as a sinner before God on certain matters. Each time, the whole meeting broke out into the praise chorus and I had to wait until they had finished before I could resume. They did not burst into song over my careful exposition of Scripture (though doubtless that was appreciated), but they did when I gave testimony as a sinner to God's forgiveness and cleansing on up-to-date matters. It was as if they said, "He knows how to repent and find what he needs at the cross—he is one of us." It was a humbling experience to be thus rejoiced over.

God did marvels among us. It seemed the Holy Spirit was absolutely free in that atmosphere of praise, and nothing was impossible. The next day was Sunday, and at 9:00 A.M. we had the usual Church of England service, somewhat shortened to allow more time for the messages, of which there were two. The African Rural Dean, who was in charge of both that church and the whole area, read the service. It was wonderful that he had been willing for the revival conference to be held on his premises at all. He came to all the meetings and seemed to show real interest. The previous day he had uttered one very significant sentence. One of us had been giving his testimony and he asked, "Did it take you long to be broken?"

We thought God was working in his heart, but we hardly dared hope for what actually happened that Sunday morning. At the close of the service, clothed in cassock and surplice, he came forward to say a few words. Many of the messages had been along the line of Jesus' bringing people out of the prison of sin. To our astonishment the African Rural Dean said by interpretation, "I have been one of Satan's jailors all this time, looking after his prisoners. But the prisoners have all escaped. So I have decided to accept the Lord Jesus and be saved too." The church echoed again and again with praise to God. Some semblance of order was established, while the clergy proceeded down the aisle into the vestry to disrobe. Outside the Africans sang, "Tukutendereza." When he appeared, he was surrounded by the happy, rejoicing crowd, embraced by numberless Africans, and then swept along to his house. When a man is unbroken and unwilling to bend, the Africans are silent, and it is quite clear that he is not in fellowship. But the moment he repents, their love knows no bound—even to a rural Dean! That afternoon some of the missionaries visited him, and he asked them to join him in prayer. He poured out his heart to God and told Him that that day he was but a newborn babe. This was indeed a notable victory for the Lord Jesus. The news of it was likely to shake deeply the forces of those who opposed the revival.

Later that morning I saw another rejoicing crowd, praising for yet another trophy: a notorious backslider had returned to the Lord. God had greatly used him in the early days, but he had gone back into sin and for years had been hard and unwilling to yield. But that day he had given in, and there was yet another to welcome back into the kingdom.

At dinner-time one day in the European marquee, Bill Butler was giving a word of thanks to the various people who had helped with all the work—it was the last day. The African cook was due for our thanks, and he was brought in and we gave him a good clap. Bill said to us in English, "He is not saved yet, but if only he served the Lord as faithfully as he has served us, he would make a good brother." Then he translated what he had said into Luganda for him, to which the cook replied that he decided there and then to accept the Lord Jesus as Savior—and this was from a man who had long withstood Him. The tent was filled with praise, and from all sides people came forward to embrace him—among them the young African king of Bugufe, who had himself been saved some years before. What a sight it was, to see a king embracing a cook! What a demonstration of the fact that at the cross men of all ranks are made one!

In the evening of that day, a friend and myself walked up to the African quarters, hoping to take a photograph of a crowd of singing Africans. We found a crowd singing all right, and by the waving of their arms we knew there must be another victory for the Lord Jesus. In their midst was a woman giving her testimony. It was the Rural Dean's wife—she had just bowed her will to the Lord Jesus and been saved. Oh, how we praised the Lamb with our African brothers. God was at work everywhere, not only in the meetings, but wherever groups of Christians were rejoicing and testifying.

In nearly all these cases there was much that the newly saved one would have to put right. The sin was often flagrant and willful. But the public manner of their welcome into the kingdom committed them all the more definitely to make the necessary restitutions. And I was told they would be lovingly held to it by their watchful African brethren.

The conversion of such people was, in a sense, incidental to the main purpose of the gathering. This was a conference of leaders in revival that they might go deeper with the Lord. But the message was so simple and inescapable that the unsaved ones among us were able to apply it to themselves and respond to the Lord.

Joe Church had drawn on a blackboard a picture of a little man languishing in prison with his indictment hanging on the wall above him. But the indictment, did he but know it, had been taken out of the way by Jesus and nailed to His cross. For that reason the door of the prison was wide open and the little man could be free if he was willing to bend his neck—the door was a low one—and repent. All the other messages and testimonies from the platform seemed to be based upon this picture, or fitted in with it. Although most of us were experienced Christians, the Lord worked so deeply in our hearts that many of us, black and white, saw the various prisons in which we had been living—prisons of bitterness and resentment, of complaining and self-pity, of lack of love or fear of others, and so on. Many came to the low door opened by the blood of Jesus and were set free to walk with Him. Testimonies to that effect were being given all the time in the smaller groups. As the Lord was applying His Word to us, the unsaved among us applied it to themselves and were converted.

This sort of thing is happening in an ever-widening circle in East Africa, and not only in special conferences such as this one. Men and women are constantly being saved, not through great preachers or big campaigns, but through the convincing testimony of a fellowship of saved sinners. Whether the fellowship is large or small, all the time the saints are going deeper in repentance and the song of praise is going up, and all the time sinners are being brought to the Lord Jesus and the fellowship increased. And the impressive thing is that nowhere has their spiritual movement left the church, usually in those parts the Anglican Church. Had similar blessing come to England or America, there would have been twenty new sects by now, all vying with each other—and that, of course, would have meant the end of revival. But in the goodness of God this revival has continued right up to the present.

There is no reason why revival should not be continuous, as long as Jesus never ceases to be Jesus. There is only one thing that quenches the Spirit and causes the blessing among the saints to halt, and that is sin. If this movement of revival has continued for so long, it is only because the brethren there have learned continually to repent and to have recourse to that blood which has power to cleanse from all those things that would otherwise cause God to "shut up heaven that there be no rain."

Thirteen

The Way Up Is Down

FROM THE FOREGOING it might seem that those of us who had been met by the Lord at such a low point in our lives and ministries had now been lifted up to walk in all the glories of revival. That would not be altogether true. For me, I found that, concurrently with all that I have just described, a process had begun in my life that was to be both painful and humiliating. It has often been said that in the Christian life God's way up is down; I found God really meant it, and that I was to go down and down more than I had ever anticipated.

I have already quoted Joe Church's expression, that revival is not the roof blowing off, but the bottom falling out. God was intent that for this strong, apparently successful evangelist it really should fall out, that He might ultimately build him up on another foundation altogether. I discovered that this was not a matter of just repenting here and getting right there; there was a bigger issue than that. The proud, stiff-necked "I" had to learn to bow its head and die in a deeper way than could ever happen in just one conference. Madame Guyon put it this way, that the life of nature has to be brought to death, if we are to be possessed by the Divine Life. And God knew how much of my service had been done merely in the strength of nature.

In *The Calvary Road* I had written words that were far deeper than I knew then and were more prophetic for me than I realized.

But dying to self is not a thing we do once for all. There may be an initial dying when God first shows us these things, but ever after, it will be a constant dying, for only so can the Lord Jesus be revealed constantly through us. . . . Every humiliation, everyone who tries and vexes us, is God's way of breaking us, so that there is a yet deeper channel in us for the life of Christ. You see, the only life that pleases God and that can be victorious is His life—never our life, no matter how hard we try. But inasmuch as our self-centered life is the exact opposite of His, we can never be filled with His life, unless we are prepared for God to bring ours constantly to death. And in that we must cooperate by our moral choice.

There is an occupational hazard for all preachers and writers; it is that when they have preached or written on some aspect of the Christian life, such as obedience, prayer, giving, dying to self, they assume that they have thereby done those things. They may not have done them at all; they may have only preached or written about them. James tells us that we may be only hearers of the Word and not doers of it, and we may add that we may also be preachers and writers of it, without doing it. The message of the book I had written was about to catch up with me, and I would have to walk the Calvary road in earnest.

Someone has said that an experience of the cross is when God's will crosses ours and we choose God's. That will comes to us not only in His Word, but in His providences, that is, in the things that He permits to enter our lives. I was about to experience a succession of them, things that certainly crossed what I would naturally have chosen for myself. I struggled against them at the time, but I ultimately had to submit to them as being permitted by God and therefore His will for me. I see them now as crosses on which I had to die that I might live again the more in Him—the old principle of "dying to live."

First of all, the experience of seeing myself as I really was and embarking on the road of repentance was so traumatic that I lost the confidence and boldness I used to have in my evangelistic work. Perhaps I was questioning myself too much; but whatever it was, I seemed to be losing the gift of the evangelist which is referred to in Ephesians 4:11, and which I had known previously in abundant measure. I remember being embarrassed when someone said to me, "I presume that the experience of revival you speak of has meant that your evangelistic work has become just so much more fruitful in the salvation of souls," and I had to confess it had not. I can see now that my life and ministry were going through a complete reorientation, that God was stripping from them the accretions that had grown up over the years and reducing them to basics, that I might begin again on the ground of grace alone. In the process I found myself sometimes ministering in two voices, one pre-revival and the other post-revival. In one evangelistic campaign some Christians came up to me and asked, "When are you going to speak again on the theme you did the other night, which touched and melted us Christians so much?" In another campaign someone said to me, "Can you tell me, are you preaching to the unsaved, or to Christians, because I want to know about bringing my converted friends?" Yes, I was going through a painful process of reorientation, and I have the impression that most of the others in that early team were too. It was not to be the work of a day.

Since then I have seen others, who have been brought to the cross[1] in a new way, go through a similar process of reorientation of their ministries, a process which has sometimes seemed to go on and on. I have hated to see the pain of it, and in sympathy with a brother have said, "Oh, God, how long?" But we all emerged ultimately not only with a new experience in our hearts, but with a brand-new message on our lips, which really was good news for bad people. We had seen ourselves as bad people, preachers that we were, and we were able to offer the same good news that we had experienced to others, whether unsaved or Christians. Further, we found that this was the theme or Scripture everywhere and we had acquired a fresh gospel theology that arose out of our sinfulness acknowl-

---

[1]Expressions such as "being brought to the cross" and "coming to the foot of the cross" appear a number of times from this point on, and I hasten to explain what is meant lest they are thought to be mere clichés. As the cross of our Lord Jesus Christ was only made necessary by human sin, to come to the cross means to take one's place as a sinner over specific matters and to confess our sin as having crucified the Lord of glory. Then, inasmuch as in His cross Jesus finished the judgment of sin on our behalf, the expression also means to enter by faith into the peace and liberty that He obtained for us there. These are also the two senses in which the expression is used in our gospel hymnology.

edged at the foot of the cross. We had to see, then, that God
was not teaching us something that would merely be an addition to our already "good" ministry, an extra arrow in our
quiver, but He was rather wanting to bring it all to death that
we might begin again as sinners on the ground of grace. As He
did this, we found that what He taught us previously came to
life again, but suffused with all the new insights and experiences of the grace of God.

This was a small trial compared with what was to come. Not
everyone said to us, "When are you going to speak again on
those themes that melt the heart?" Many wanted to hear no
more of it. Indeed, the message of revival by which we had
profited so much caused something of a controversy in evangelical circles in Britain. It was quite extraordinary how quickly it
became a talking point among Christian leaders from one end
of the country to the other, and we were thought to have "gone
off the rails," the principle charge being that we were making
people overly introspective. Thus we found ourselves all at
once the objects of criticism from a number of quarters, and I
more than the other brethren because, whereas they were
ministers known in the main only to their congregations, as an
evangelist I was known all over the country. As a result I
became *persona non grata* in circles where before I had always
been welcomed as a speaker. This was not easy to bear, but for
me it was part of "the bottom falling out" and, because it was
humbling, very good for my soul! In spite of all this, the circle
of our fellowship continued to expand, many a sinking Christian desperately grasped the life line of grace that we threw out
to him, and the annual holiday conferences in North Wales
were blessed by the Lord beyond anything we deserved and
continued to attract hungry-hearted Christians.

It may well be asked why there should have been this
opposition? First, people found it surprising to hear an
evangelist take the sinner's place over his present condition
and give testimony to new forgiveness and cleansing. Whereas
this melted and helped some, it frankly shocked others. Some
of my brethren in the ministry found the same reaction in their
churches when they began to share their experiences. The
minister or the evangelist was not supposed to be wrong in
anything; the people would much prefer him to remain on his

pedestal; they found it embarrassing to see him come off it— indeed they hated it. In some churches, however, that was the day when conviction of sin came upon the people.

Secondly, the message was so practical and so closely applied that people instinctively felt that under it God was going to take them to pieces in order to put them together again, and they did not appreciate the thought. There had been the same fear of, and opposition to, revival in East Africa, where, of course, both revival and opposition were on a much larger scale. There was a time when the missions there had been split right down the middle in their attitude toward the revival movement. There had been all sorts of rationalizations as to the reasons for that opposition, but at bottom much of it was simply fear of its personal challenge. For ourselves we knew we had had the same reactions at first and therefore could not point the finger.

There was yet another reason, something in which we ourselves were at fault. An element of law had entered our message; we were not actually saying, or rather implying, "This do and thou shalt live" as at Sinai, but we *were* implying, "This do and thou shalt have revival." It was only a slight element of law, but a little leaven was enough to leaven the whole lump and make us quite unacceptable to some, though they could not always identify what it was that made them uneasy. But with hindsight I can see this was the underlying cause of the opposition. This related especially to certain aspects of truth, about which I will speak later. This sometimes made our message sound formularized and our testimony *gauche:* law is always *gauche;* only grace is spontaneous and free, and there was much that we were yet to learn of the way of grace. Here I must speak just for myself; being the man I am, I know I could not have found my way to a new understanding and experience of spiritual things without making some such mistakes. But I was not going to let the fear of doing so prevent me from pressing on. So I just had to accept all that was coming to me.

All of us made mistakes, often along the line of being goaded by conscience rather than guided by the Spirit. But we were learning not only to bear one another's burdens but also one another's reproach. If ever any of us began to deny our identification with a brother because of other people's criticism of him, we repented and our oneness continued.

I learned this especially at a campaign I was conducting in a church in one of England's great university cities, at the invitation of a local committee there. I had invited a friend of mine, a leader in a nearby church and one who had been touched in the same way that I had, to give his testimony one night. In the prayer meeting beforehand he was praying with great earnestness that he should be willing to be known for what he really was. Quite obviously what he thought he should say was going to be very costly to him. In the event it proved that he was being goaded rather than guided, for he shared things that should not have been mentioned in public, things to do with sex that had happened before he was a Christian. Realizing the shock that this was causing, Revel gesticulated to me from the piano to stop him. As I sat there, I realized the criticism that this would cause and how I would be involved. Then suddenly I recalled a letter which I had received but a few days before from Lawrence Barham, written from the boat as he was returning to East Africa. He had said, "Roy, it needs someone in England to take responsibility for the mistakes people will make in finding the highway." It dawned on me that that was just what I was having to do, and I said to myself, "What a privilege!"

That incident ricocheted over England for years to come and perhaps closed some doors against me, because I was identified with him. So be it, I said to myself. I saw the mistake as clearly as any, but he was my brother and who was I to dissociate myself from him? How was I to know that I might not be the next to "drop a brick"? In those days God seemed to give us a carefree spirit to stand together, weather the storm, learn from our mistakes and live them all down. We were Mephibosheths indeed, "lame on both our feet," but by grace we were sitting at the King's table, even as he sat at David's. As our message was for other Mephibosheths, we seemed to qualify to speak to them of that grace if only by our very weaknesses.

I was to feel the edge of this opposition in a yet sharper way. In 1948 I had left the service of the National Young Life Campaign to accept a position of leadership in another splended interdenominational society, which would afford me even larger opportunities for evangelistic campaigns. So we had moved to the Greater London area. But soon critical comments began coming to the committee concerning the ministry of the man they had appointed, all along the lines I have already indicated. More than once I would return home from a campaign where God had worked in saving souls and blessing His people to find a letter from the committee, summoning me before them. We spent long hours together, trying to find common ground, and I sought to give them every assurance. But they found it difficult to verbalize what they felt, for what was thought to be wrong was all rather subtle. In the end, in 1950 to be precise, they asked for my resignation after just two years with them, and I think they were right to do so. Their society had been brought into being for a certain line of work and they had to ensure that it proceeded on that line without impediment.

This was not quite the blow that it might have been. Soon after I had joined them, even before there was any trouble, the Lord showed me that I was wrong ever to have left the former movement and that only an ambitious spirit had prompted me to make the change. Moreover, it meant that I was now free to accept the invitation to go to Uganda for the great revival conference described in the previous chapter, which was just the encouragement I needed at that time.

However, this corn of wheat was to "fall into the ground and die" in an even deeper way; only so could it ultimately bring forth any fruit. On getting back from Uganda I received an invitation, quite unsought from a committee in the north of England supported by a number of evangelical churches, to be the evangelist in their county, where the people had been particularly bereft of gospel ministry. I prayed earnestly and asked the advice of my brethren, as I was anxious not to make another false step. There was nothing in the circumstances to give me any indication one way or the other, neither did any word come from the Lord. Ultimately I felt I must accept, as it offered every opportunity to preach the gospel and would provide my support. A date was set for a welcome meeting and certain campaigns lined up. I gave a month's notice to our landlord that we were giving up our apartment in the London area; Revel was to remain there for that period, while I commuted up and down to the North until we could move up there.

The first meeting seemed a great occasion. One person after another welcomed me and spoke about "this man of God whom He has used so greatly in the past and whom we trust He will continue to use in our midst." I gave a first message then and a further message in one of the sessions during the half-night of prayer that followed. That was enough so to alarm the committee as to cause them to get together as soon as they could to discuss the ministry of this man, who at this first utterance had called the Christians to repent of their sins and get right with God and had even told of his own experience of repentance. No doubt my presentation was not adequately balanced, and I expect there was something of striving in my own strength on that occasion, but it seemed incredible that there should be such a swift reaction after all the fine-sounding things that had just been said.

A further test was that when I arrived in the North I found that the financial support was very different from what I had assumed, much less than was needed, since we had a son to maintain at boarding school. This would mean that we would have to send him to a local state school. Then I discovered that a house was provided for us at Jarrow, an industrial town on the northeast coast, and at that time one of the most deprived and depressed areas in the whole country—Michael would have to be brought up and go to school there, and I feared a boy in such a school might have to leave at fourteen. Gone would be any idea of his going to a university and into a profession.

I had foolishly not made inquiries into the financial side before accepting the post. All this was a heavy blow indeed, and I really suffered at the prospect. I remember going past a cemetery in those parts one day and, looking at the graves, I said to myself, "They are in a happier position than I am, for 'there the wicked cease from troubling and the weary are at rest.'" I had never got so low as to say this before, nor have I since. I was reading at the time Mrs. Penn-Lewis's book on Job, and it offered me some comfort. But one night in bed, as all the implications dawned on me, I sat up and prayed, "You can't mean it, Lord, You can't."

"Can't I?" He seemed to reply. "Cannot I do what I will with Mine own?"

After a struggle, at about midnight, I bowed my neck to the yoke He was offering me and I said, "So be it, Lord."

That was Saturday night; the following Sunday proved an amazing day of preaching for me. All day long I was near to tears in the pulpit, not because of self-pity, but because all the time He was putting His arms around me, caressing me. In every hymn we sang, in every prayer we prayed, and in every Scripture we read He spoke of His love for me.

I said, "Lord, if You don't stop, I shall burst into tears before all these people."

Nothing touches the Lord and draws out His sympathy so much as when He sees us accepting some severe cross, and He pours His love upon us. He knows, too, how to put a thousand cushions and compensations around us to make His burden light and His yoke easy when we submit.

I had to read in one of the services that day the trial of Jesus Christ and the verdict pronounced upon Him, and I knew instinctively the result of that committee. And so it happened. They gave me three months' salary and bade me go.

Thus I was spared having to bring my family there and rob my son of the education we had planned. But I was glad I was made willing first.

In all this God was getting Revel and me where He wanted us. How could I blame the men involved when, as it proved, they were the instruments of His guidance? It became clear to us that we were not called to work with a society or a committee, but to be free to work according to the vision of revival He had given us along with our brethren, even if it meant looking to God direct for our income.

The strange thing, indeed the beautiful thing, was that the incident left no bitterness. When I went to Jamaica years later, one of the principle members of that committee, by then the pastor of the large Baptist church in Kingston, warmly invited me to preach for him.

However, the eviction from this post in the north of England led to a further experience of the cross which was rather more painful. I went to my landlord in Beckenham to tell him we were staying on in the apartment after all. He said that was impossible as he had already signed up another tenant. To appreciate what a grievous blow this was to us, you have to understand that in the 1950s in Britain there was a great shortage of rented accommodation either houses or apartments. We found ourselves facing a deadline by which to leave, but having nowhere to go. Our brethren rallied round and we searched everywhere, but to no avail. At that time I had to be away for a week on a campaign. I made daily telephone calls to Revel to ascertain how things were going, only to hear her crying sometimes at the other end of the line. Immediately afterward I had to compose myself and go into a meeting and try to preach a buoyant gospel message! So often domestic crises hit the evangelist when he is away from home in the midst of public ministry. Many a minister of a church has the same hard time, bearing a heavy personal cross while having to present a composed image in public.

Eventually we accepted the invitation of Fred and Constance Barff, two of the closest to us on the team, to make our home with them in their vicarage in Bristol. This was not just a rescue operation on their part. This was what they had wanted ever since they knew of our plight, bless them, chiefly because they saw in it the opportunity of our working out together in fellowship the new lessons we had been learning. We, too, valued the prospect, but it was hard to contemplate not having a place of our own, with a boy coming home from boarding school. When we arrived in Bristol with all our belongings, the Barffs, through no fault of their own, had to be out. That night Revel and I cried ourselves to sleep in that gaunt vicarage.

Thus the Lord brought us down to the place where we had no home of our own, no on-going income and, hardest of all, no opportunities of service for the Lord such as I had known. Just three years before, every door was open to me as an evangelist; now every one was closed right across Britain. And this applied also to Bristol, a city where a few years ago before I had had one of the mightiest tent campaigns of my experience.

The criticism against us as a group and of myself in particular was at its height. The news that I had been asked to leave two reputable evangelical societies because of the message I was preaching was enough to make me highly suspect in the churches. I felt as if I was the "naughty boy" of the evangelicals.

Revel confessed to me that she sometimes feared to go out of the house lest she should meet someone who was critical of us, and she had to bring that fear to the Lord. All I could do was to go around to the churches of the brethren, the slowly growing number of ministers who had had a new meeting with the Lord, and give the Word there and encourage the small fellowship groups that had begun to spring up. There was something else I should do, Fred Barff always insisted, and that was to learn deeper brokenness and fellowship with them at the vicarage. He never doubted that that was the main reason why God had brought us to be with them.

I was encouraged to remember that my dear friend and brother, William Nagenda, had had much the same experience in Uganda when he and several others were expelled from the theological college at Mukono, just because of the stigma of revival, and were forbidden to preach in any of the churches. There was nothing left for him to do but to witness for Jesus on the buses. Yet the way down for him had become the way up into a wide, fruitful ministry, and I could only hope it would somehow be the same for me. But sometimes I hardly dared hope and would lie awake at night, saying to myself, "Too old at forty, too old at forty." Then I had to repent of "tempting God in the wilderness" by entertaining low thoughts of His love and power, and ask His forgiveness.

One great gain was that I was relieved of trying to do two things at the same time, attempting to continue as the strong evangelist and also undergo a complete reorientation. I could stop and begin again at the beginning; I could unlearn what I had to unlearn and allow God to give me a new message and ministry, based on grace alone, without having to maintain the old simultaneously.

Not that we were inactive. Far from it. There were conferences here and there, and, of course, there was the organizing of our annual holiday conference. But it was all on a small scale; it was basically a learning time. The marvel was that, although what I was doing did not seem greatly productive by human standards, the Lord maintained us financially—I hardly remember how at this distance. I once said to Revel, "The Lord has sent us back to school—and do you know what? He is paying our school fees!"

Very soon we were to go even lower. God was intent on doing a thorough work, so that we should be in no doubt that it was He who was dealing with us. Before these troubles had reached their height, Revel had become pregnant and we were looking forward to an addition to our family after the long period since Michael was born. But it had been a troubled pregnancy and there had been a series of threatened miscarriages. I had just got back to the Barffs' vicarage from meetings in France, when she had a massive hemorrhage, leading up to what is called *eclampsia*. She was rushed to the hospital, and the baby was removed, dead, as a life-saving measure. But the kidneys had been so damaged that they had ceased to work. As she lay there unconscious with a glucose drip-tube in her nose, the surgeon said to me, "That is all we can do. If those kidneys begin to work again, then she will recover; if they don't, in a short while it will be the end."

It had been blow after blow, down, down, down until it had come to this. "O sword of the Lord, how long will it be ere thou be quiet." It was the fact that all these things had happened in such rapid succession and that they were all leading in one direction—down—that made me know it was God and not chance. No one but He could have done it. This fact, strangely, comforted me. If we were being squeezed, they were His fingers that were doing it, the fingers of the One who loved us both, and it made me feel safe. I found I would infinitely prefer to be squeezed by Him than to be caressed by the world, or even by the church. I felt like saying with David, "Let us now fall into the hands of the Lord; for His mercies are great: and let me not fall into the hand of man." We had previously fallen into the hands of man; now we had fallen directly into the hands of God, and we were to prove indeed how great were His mercies.

If God's chastening hand had been heavy on me, and if test after test had come in relentless succession, things came right one by one just as quickly when He lifted His hand. In no time at all, it seemed, the skies were blue over my head—it was quite extraordinary. It was just an instance of the working out of the ancient word, "For a small moment have I forsaken thee, but with great mercies will I gather thee; in a little wrath I hid my face for a moment, but with everlasting kindness will I have mercy on thee."

The process of chastening and testing had appeared unrelieved and endless, but it was only "for a small moment" as God saw it. It is how we act in that "small moment" that is of such importance. To change the metaphor and to use one taken from the English game of cricket, we can't score runs unless we are bowled against. The fast bowling may not be pleasant to stand up to, but when it ceases, gone is our opportunity to score runs, that is, to demonstrate unshaken faith that God is for us. I cannot claim to have scored many runs at that time, but when I failed to stand up to the bowling, I repented; the blood of Christ covered my doubts and wrong reactions, and my faith in that blood was counted to me for righteousness. And in the end I had good cause to praise Him that "His anger endureth but for a moment, His favor for a lifetime."

First of all, He gave Revel back to me right from the gates of death. The news of her danger traveled, I know not how, all over the country and to other countries, even to East Africa; and it was as if God blew His trumpet and called forth His prayer forces to withstand Satan, that he should go no further than the limits God had permitted him. Without any organizing on man's part, so many people were drawn to pray in groups and in other ways that the number must have run into four figures. So deep was the concern in the hospital that the Christian nurses gathered there for special prayer. The workers in the maternity wards hated more than anything else to lose a mother, and for the Christians this one was their sister.

God was gracious; the kidneys began to work again, her eyesight returned (the *eclampsia* had affected her eyes), and she began to make a slow and steady recovery. During that time of distress I humbled myself and repented before God of certain sins I had been "going easy on." As I had been seeing much those days of the power of the blood of Christ, not only to cleanse sin, but to make good all that had resulted from it by way of difficulty and discipline, I used to say of Revel that God had "brought her again from the dead by the blood of the everlasting covenant." As I drove to the hospital each day I found myself singing one verse of a hymn again and again.

> Pining souls, come nearer Jesus,
> And oh, come not doubting thus;
> But with faith that trusts more bravely
> His huge tenderness for us.

I saw anew that "huge tenderness," I rested my head on it, trusted it, and knew our affairs were safe in His hands, no matter how they might appear.

Then God did yet another apparently impossible thing. He gave us a home of our own in Bristol, a precious flat to rent, something we had almost despaired of, and that through a series of links that only He could have forged. When Revel ultimately came out of the hospital, I brought her with joy into our new home, everything bright and shining and with all the furniture in position; and her eyes, still weak, blinked at the brightness and wonder of it. We were to spend seven happy years in that home, until we moved back to London. Revel herself was given in all another sixteen years, years which proved wonderfully fruitful as she shared with me in the work and developed her own unique ministry which blessed many on both sides of the Atlantic. When she did go to heaven in 1967 it was by another route altogether.

Then the Lord made us content to be in Bristol and nowhere else, and happy to accept just the openings He gave to spread His message. They were not the large united campaigns of former days, but they were even more meaningful perhaps, as teams of us took small conferences here and there. Occasionally we were presented with larger opportunities, as when Lawrence Barham and Bill Butler joined me on one of their furloughs to conduct a campaign in the Civic Hall, Sheffield. Then I found myself often being called to Alsace and Switzerland, where rivers of revival had begun to flow, and I had the new and exciting experience of preaching by interpretation, and where we saw the Lord do beautiful things. Then each summer there was the Holiday Conference which drew together all those who had a hunger for the "new and living way," the number of which was growing year by year.

God was indeed drying my tears and giving me "everlasting consolation and good hope through grace."

Fourteen

Jesus in the Center

IN THE FOLLOWING year, 1952, I entered at last upon what I can only call the golden years. It was in that year that the Lord began to deal with that element of law which had entered my message and that of my brothers and to bring us all much more into the sunlight of grace, thus making the message of revival simpler to us than ever before. God did so by the return to England of our Ugandan brother, William Nagenda. Five years before he had been one of the original team from East Africa who had toured the country, proclaiming the need of repentance and the power of the blood of Christ. When he returned, he saw that we who had been helped through the former visit had been caught in a subtle bondage and he addressed almost all his ministry to meet this need.

As this was one of the most crucial things in our lives, I must explain how it came about that we were in any bondage at all.

When the first group of missionaries had come to England, they had summarized what they had learned under five heads. We, of course, listened with the greatest of interest to discover the secret and we virtually ticked off each point. First, prayer with a hunger. I knew all about praying for revival; the secret could not lie there. Then, brokenness. That was not new either, I thought; it was the same as death to sin—Romans 6 and all that—which I had been preaching for years, but without experiencing revival. Then, the fullness of the Spirit. The secret, I felt, could not lie there either, for Keswick had preached it for years and so had I, but without revival. Then they came to openness, which they based on 1 John 1:7, "If we walk in the light, as He is in the light, we have fellowship one with another, and the blood of Jesus Christ, His Son, cleanseth us from all sin." This "walking in the light" they defined as the willingness to know and be known.

Here was a new challenge to my heart. I was not always willing to know the truth about myself as God would show it me, and as for willingness to be known as I really was, I was far from that. I was a closed book; not even my wife knew me as I really was. And if such openness leads to the fifth point, oneness, little wonder that I had so few deep relationships with others. These were two points I could not tick off.

Because "walking in the light" was a new challenge, we tended to think that here was the missing secret, and very subtly the attempt to be open about ourselves with others came to occupy a more prominent place than it should. The fact that it was costly made us feel all the more that it was essential, an integral part of brokenness. As a result it became almost a law to us, and our fellowship became formularized. I remember I used to have sometimes two battles when it came to repentance: first, to call a thing sin and confess it to the Lord; second, to share this with someone else—as if somehow it was mandatory to do so.

On one occasion I asked one of the original team to what extent was it necessary to share all that went on in one's heart with another. He gave me no clear answer to that question, but left me to my conscience. I suppose he did not want to let me off any challenge God might be giving me, knowing that naturally we all prefer to hide sin and walk in darkness. But conscience, unless it is well instructed by the Holy Spirit, is not an adequate guide and has a natural tendency to legalism. Because sometimes a confession to another is clearly prompted by the Holy Spirit, as seen by the good that comes of it, conscience will always tend to make a law out of the experience and cause us to feel we must be ever after confessing to another, and will condemn us if we do not. If only that brother had as much as hinted that such legalism was a possibility, it might have saved me from doing a number of mistaken things in which I was goaded by conscience rather than guided by the Spirit. But the team from East Africa were, on their own confession, as much learning and finding their feet on the highway of holiness as we were in England.

It must be understood that our position was not as clearly defined to us at that time as I now describe it after the passage of years. Looking back is like taking a picture with a telescopic lens in which the distance between images, one behind another, seems eliminated and they all crowd on top of one another. It was not, therefore, bondage all the time by any means; God often used the openness of our testimonies to break many before Him and to sweep them into a new life. The fellowship in our summer Holiday Conference was often utterly heavenly. It was just as an element of law that had entered. But when William Nagenda came back, he spotted it and declared it a dangerous one. Indeed, he went so far as to say, not only that we had made too much of "walking in the light" and such like, but that we had put it in the center where Jesus should have been.

In 1952 William spent the whole four weeks of the Holiday Conference with us, and throughout he gave us corrective ministry, so much so that it seemed to silence the rest of the English team. This meant he was invariably the one who had to give the messages, which was as hard for him as it was for us. His theme was almost always the same. He used a large Thompson Chain-Reference Bible, in the center of which, on the cover, he had stuck a white circular spot to which he would point again and again and say, "It is not walking in the light in the center, nor brokenness, nor some formula, but Jesus in the center." He went so far as to say repeatedly, "and not *Calvary Road* in the center," for he feared lest a formula could be deduced from it which would get in the center.

It can be understood how puzzling it was for us to hear him demoting the very things which we felt we had learned from him in the first place years before. But if he seemed to knock such phrases as brokenness and walking in the light, he was more broken than any; he virtually lived at the cross, knowing constant cleansing from all sorts of selfish reactions. More than this, he was walking in the light himself as much as any; he was as transparent as a child in our fellowship; we could read him

like a book and he wanted us to. Yet he never ceased to insist
that life was found in none of these things, but only in Jesus. If
these things were regarded as necessary steps into blessing,
they could lead us to striving and bondage, whereas Jesus sets
men free. We had to see that Jesus in the midst was Himself
revival, that God had no more to give than Him, and that when
He was in the center, then brokenness, openness, testimony,
and fellowship followed as natural effects of the great First
Cause. The secret lay in none of the five points considered by
themselves, but only in Christ Himself. Had it been presented
to us in that way at the first, we might have ticked that off
quicker than some of the other points, as something we already
knew which had not produced revival.

This was exactly what burdened William. He was given a
holy and apostolic jealousy for Jesus, and he never tired of
casting down every high thing, every emphasis that exalted
itself against Him and the grace embodied in Him for sinners.
He used to say that he was quite sure that if the average
Christian went into a library and saw many books with a wide
variety of titles on Christian topics and one among them
marked just *Jesus*, it would be the one book they would pass by
in their search for victory and revival. And yet only in that One
was to be found the fullness of the Godhead, revival, and
everything else. Indeed, he who had seen and known so much
of revival in East Africa could hardly bear to use the term, lest it
should take the place of Jesus in the center.

This at first sight seemed to lead us back to square one where
we had been before we started five years previously. The most
unrevived Christian could easily agree that the Christian life
was just walking with Jesus and would claim he was doing so.
We saw, however, that if a Christian is supposedly walking
with Him and yet is playing with sin, out of fellowship with
others, always regarding himself as right, never repenting and
never sharing his heart with others, then the Jesus he thinks he
is walking with is a false Jesus. The real Jesus is full not only of
grace but of truth, too: "His eyes are as a flame of fire, and His
feet like unto fine brass . . . and His voice as the sound of many
waters."

When we put Him in the center and allow Him really to
"walk in the midst of the seven golden candlesticks," He

cannot but say sometimes, "I have somewhat against thee . . .
be zealous therefore and repent." He cannot but call upon us to
get right with our brother and love him as we have been loved,
and we in our turn want to share with others the new experiences of His forgiveness and cleansing. He is the First Cause.
We walk in the light only because He "is light and in Him is no
darkness at all." We are broken only because the One we are
walking with is the Broken One, meek and lowly in heart. We
get right with our brother and love him only because He the
infinite loving One is in the center and shows us when our
attitudes are those of love.

I have to confess that at first I did not appreciate the challenge that William Nagenda brought. Whatever the matter in
question, most of us have a hard time confessing ourselves to
be wrong, such is our love for our own righteousness, and I was
no exception. I resented the challenge and criticized Willian
for it. But eventually I could only agree with God, and I saw it
all; I had indeed been putting something else in the center, but
Jesus Himself now took that place and we all moved into a new
experience of liberation. J. B. Phillips's translation of Romans
10:4 summed up for us what we were seeing: "Christ means the
end of the struggle for righteousness by the law for everyone
who believes in Him." Not only was He the end of the struggle
for righteousness (that is, a right relationship with God) by the
law, but the end of the struggle for peace by the law and for
power by the law—and we saw especially, for revival by the
law. As sinners at the foot of the cross we had come to the end of
our struggle for revival: there where we confessed failure. He
became for us all our revival and everything else we needed.
One gospel song became our special favorite:

> Jesus Christ is made to me
>   All I need, all I need;
> He alone is all my plea,
>   He is all I need;
> Wisdom, righteousness and power,
> Holiness this very hour,
> My redemption full and sure;
>   He is all I need.

Strangely, this did not mean less repentance and openness

among us but rather more, because we were now under grace. And under grace we could afford to acknowledge ourselves as sinners, for as such we qualified the more for Jesus. As Revel put it once when she tried to summarize what God had shown her, "I have had a new sight of the character of God whereby I can afford to be real." Furthermore, the manner of our actual sharing and fellowship was under grace. It was the blood of Christ that put us right with God, and not merely confessing to one another. That blood alone was enough. This meant that the repenting one had a testimony to give because of the power of the blood, but he was under no obligation to give it except as God guided. This meant that the "heat was off" us and we were free.

All this resulted in a simpler, deeper, and more liberating note in what we had to offer others, and joy flowed like a river. This is what revival is all about. Revival is not merely the saints weeping under conviction or the saints repenting in brokenness, but ultimately and supremely it is the saints rejoicing and made happy in their God.

As I look back and see my pilgrimage in perspective, I would say that what the Lord showed me at that time proved a far more important turning point than even the occasion five years before when He brought me back to the cross and began to revive my spiritual life. I thought I had found it all then and even wrote *The Calvary Road*, but it was not actually until five years later that the Lord brought me into the freedom of grace.

More than that, it was only then that the Lord allowed Revel and me to go to the United States of America for the first time, a land that has meant so much to me since. Had we gone before, we would have gone with a message that was not clear on grace, just that bit lopsided, and people might have gotten tied up rather than set free. As it was, we went with nothing but the simple gospel message, applying it to the deeper needs of Christians. Under that message of grace people could not but be blessed and set free.

Furthermore, by acknowledging the Lord Jesus as the only center, we put ourselves on the trail of ever-increasing discoveries of the grace of God. The Jesus who now took for us the central place was not what He is to so many, just another

Moses, who tells people what is right and wrong, who blesses them when they achieve the right but cannot but censure them when they do not. Such a conception of Him only makes for reproach and despair. But Jesus is the One by whom grace has come for sinners; as John 1:17 says, "The law was given by Moses" and condemned the lot of us "but grace and truth came by Jesus Christ." As grace is the love of God for those who do not deserve it, the possibilities were limitless, for God did not have to find a procuring cause in us before He could bless us. Indeed, we saw that our very wrongs made us candidates for the grace of God, provided we confessed them. To such a Jesus there was no sin too shameful for Him to forgive, no situation too far gone for Him to make good.

As we have preached this sort of message all over the world, many have listened with a sort of wonder. Revival came so much more quickly when we preached grace. This is the message that brings revival to the individual and to the church. We can preach repentance as strongly as we will, provided it is always in the context of grace; people will know then that even the message of judgment is nothing more than an offer of mercy and there will be every inducement for them to repent. But if we preach hard, stringent conditions for revival, people will feel defeated before they begin.

This discovery of the grace of God has continued, increasing in importance, right up to the present, and it has given me a new Bible. It has accounted for any blessing God has brought to empty hearts as I have traveled the world, often in team with others. And it all began in 1952 when I had to agree with God that I had put a formula in the center rather than the Lord Jesus. And that brother who challenged me, William Nagenda, and whom I so resented, became one of my dearest friends and we have gone to other countries together with the message. As I think of him today in heaven, called early into the Lord's presence, I can only say, he loved me—as he did so many others. No one has been quite able to take his place in the revival movement.

Fifteen

First Visit to America

IN 1953 REVEL AND I paid our first visit to the United States. It lasted six months, and its importance in our spiritual development was considerable. It gave us just the encouragement we needed, and other visits have followed. I have come to love that land and its people, and I regard it as my second country.

The first suggestion that Revel and I should go came from Norman Grubb, who in his time has been an encourager of many. He was at that time the international secretary of the Worldwide Evangelization Crusade and had visited Rwanda to have first-hand experience of the revival movement in East Africa. His heart responded deeply to all he saw and heard, and when he returned to America he could talk of little else. Almost everywhere he went he gave a long address lasting two hours or more, describing the lessons to be learned from that revival movement. This exactly matched the spiritual hunger among the Christians, and they longed to hear more—and followed him from place to place to hear that address again and again.

They asked him, "Is there no book with these things written down? Where can we read more?"

"The only book I know," he replied, "is Roy Hession's *Calvary Road.*"

The American branch of the Christian Literature Crusade, a sister movement of the WEC sharing the same campus, had just published the little book, and with this recommendation it began to circulate widely and went right across America. Printing after printing was called for, a task which the CLC workers undertook with their own fair hands, and sometimes they had a hard time to keep up with the calls.

Norman then wrote and asked if I would visit America, as there was such a thirst in the churches for more of this ministry. If I was willing to do so, he and his organization would gladly set up a tour. I took this invitation to Joe Church and William Nagenda, who were in England at the time, and we prayed about it. Revel and I felt that we did not want to undertake this without them. They could give only limited time to such a tour, however, whereas I had all the time needed since there were still not many doors open to me in England. It was decided that Revel and I should spend the first four months in America, to be joined by Joe and William for a further two months. "Go," said Joe. "You've had a hard time here, and I am sure you will come back encouraged."

Our base was the headquarters of WEC, a large mansion in its own grounds at Fort Washington, outside Philadelphia. Here we stayed for three weeks, ministering to the workers and conducting conferences in three churches in Philadelphia. It was a new world to us and we needed to get adjusted. For instance, the evening of our first meeting in a church in Philadelphia was a cold night with snow falling. Expecting the churches to be heated no better than they were in England, Revel went suitably attired in heavy coat, scarf, gloves, and wool-lined boots, intending to speak on the platform like that! In England, you know, we go to heaven the hard way! What was our surprise to find the church so well heated that the ladies were sitting in taffeta skirts and the men in summer suits, while their winter coats hung on stands at the rear of the church! I teased her about that for long afterward!

John Whittle, one of the WEC workers whom we knew when he lived in England, felt called to give up his other work in order to organize this tour and travel with us. We were "babes in the wood," and as first-time visitors from England we looked with awe at his American car, which seemed so large and sumptuous compared with what was normal then in Europe. But it was a wonderful asset and we traveled in much comfort from the East to the West Coast and back, as well as many deviations north and south, some ten thousand miles. We had never realized how vast it was, how the distance from New York to Los Angeles was as great as that between Southampton and New York. Our eyes popped at the new sights, and we were forever commenting on the differences between the two countries. America seemed as bright as a new penny compared with England, which had barely recovered from the effects of the war and still appeared rundown by contrast. When we got back we must have bored our English friends, as we could talk of nothing else.

The pity is that on each subsequent visit one loses much of the wonder and surprise and takes for granted things that before had provoked "oohs" and "aahs." I remember the schoolboy thrill I experienced when in Denver I saw my first rodeo, with real live cowboys riding the broncos, roping the calves, and wrestling the steers. I recall the awe with which we both looked down on the mighty Grand Canyon, that time-sculptured gorge in Arizona, a mile deep, ten miles across, and over two hundred miles long, within which there rise eroded cliffs like temples. "Golly, what a gully!" said Mark Twain when he saw it—"God, what a glory!" says the Christian.

Then there was the wonder of our first crossing of the stupendous Rocky Mountains—not so beautiful as the Swiss Alps, but so much vaster. Then there was the enjoyment of driving across the colorful Arizona desert and our first encounter with the saguaro cactus trees with their weird and infinitely various shapes. Even the first time we walked in the orange groves of California was exciting to us, groves which are now, alas, giving place to urban development. Now when we visit America we are so intent on other things that we do not "turn aside to see this (or that) great sight."

These new experiences were, however, only small bonuses thrown in by the Lord as we pursued more important ends.

We found the Christians in these churches warm-hearted and generous to a degree, and they gave us a tremendous welcome. Two things characterized the situation in contrast to Britain. First, there was a fresh, ingenuous hunger for a deeper, experiential knowledge of the Lord. The Americans seemed to tumble over themselves in their eagerness to learn the way of reality and victory, not only from us, but from

Norman Grubb and anyone else whose ministry had the ring of reality. Second, there was a ready responsiveness to the actual message we had brought, and as we gave it, we were received as angels from heaven. There was no suspicious scrutiny of it, but a simple-hearted openness to God. Ministers shared in the common hunger and we found ourselves speaking at their ministerial gatherings. When we turned to prayer after the message, it was no uncommon thing for repentance to flow all over the place in a most natural way. This contrasted sharply with the opposition we had met in England and the constant battle with criticism. Of course, the Lord had moved us on since those earlier years in England and we came supremely with the message of grace—and who wants to protect himself against that? In any case, it always steals up on us on the side where we have no defenses.

We found that *The Calvary Road* had opened more doors than we could possibly enter. Then, as people were freshly blessed in our meetings and saw grace and release even more clearly than in that book, yet more calls came. As I have continued visiting the States, I have often considered that if I was allowed another life and gave it all to America, I would still not get around to all the churches that were calling for more of this ministry.

You can understand what this did for us, coming as we did from our vale of tears in England. It melted us. encouraged us, healed our wounds, and gave us added confirmation that this was the message that the church worldwide needed, by which God planned to revive His people.

Little wonder that I have come to love that land, for it gave Revel and me what we needed at a critical time in our lives. This has been typical of the ministry of America generally. She has provided refuge, help, and opportunity for all sorts of people who have come to her shores from other lands where they have not been able to "make a go of it"—be they economically deprived, refugees from political oppression, or victims of religious persecution. Through the magic of America the plain unsuccessful have so often found opportunity and abundant success which they would never have found in their own countries. I always feel like choking when I read the words inscribed on the Statue of Liberty in New York harbor:

> Give me your tired, your poor,
> Your huddled masses yearning to breathe free,
> The wretched refuse of your teeming shore;
> Send these, the homeless, tempest-tossed, to me;
> I lift my lamp beside the golden door.

I choke because I was one of the tired and poor for whom America lifted her lamp beside the door of opportunity. Although I never thought of settling there, I owe her an undying debt, because she ministered to me as I was ministering to her. Those words move me even more when I read them as echoes of what Jesus says to a hard world: "Give Me your tired, your poor . . . the wretched refuse of earth's teeming shore." I have myself come to Him as such, and He has lifted for me His lamp beside the golden door of eternal life.

When we got to California—the Golden State—we worked our way up from San Diego and Los Angeles in the south to the "white" city of San Francisco in the north—white because on its many hills all its homes are painted white and seem to sparkle in the Californian sun. There we saw the famous Golden Gate bridge through which so many missionaries have sailed over the years to the Orient. Around the immense San Francisco Bay are great cities such as Oakland and Berkeley.

It was at Oakland we met Wesley Nelson, the minister of the Mission Covenant church there, to whom we were later to be bound in close spiritual ties. I mention him here because he opened for us doors for later tours to the churches in his denomination which he longed should hear the same message of grace—and not only for us, but also for William Nagenda and Festo Kivengere of East Africa.

At that time he was a tense, struggling Christian trying as hard as he knew how to be the minister he should be and falling under condemnation because he failed. As a result of the meetings in his church, he saw Jesus afresh and embarked on a new course of spiritual freedom. I give here his own account of what the Lord did for him at that time.

> It was when the pamphlet *Path to Power* by A. W. Tozer was placed in my hands that I first began to realize how far the average Christian experience of today falls short of normal Christian living. I was awakened then, but not released. It was years later, when, frustrated by

bondage and failure, sick in mind and heart and soul, I wished only that there was some way I could be released from the ministry, that I finally trusted God to work it all out for me. The message of *The Calvary Road,* by Roy Hession and *Continuous Revival* by Norman P. Grubb came to me like a breath of fresh air. Then Mr. and Mrs. Roy Hession came to my church. Is it presumptuous for me to believe that God sent them to America for me?[1]

I knew I ought to be a better Christian. I also knew that there were certain things that would make me a better Christian. It must be all by the grace of God. But the grace of God must be received by faith, and my faith was weak. I understood that my faith must be strengthened by feeding on the Word of God, but reading the Bible was becoming an increasingly difficult chore. It would help if I prayed more fervently for the Spirit to enlighten the Scriptures, but when I prayed my mind wandered. I needed to discipline myself, but I lacked the willpower. If I were a better Christian I would read my Bible more and pray better, my faith would be strengthened and I would be able to exercise more self-discipline. *But how could I become a better Christian when I could not do the things that would make me a better Christian?* I was caught in a vicious circle. . . .

It is a terrifying sensation to have one's religion fail one. Yet, for me, it was the best thing that could have happened, for when everything else failed, Christ stepped in and He did not fail. None of the theological truths changed, but a new significance was injected into them. I had preached a gospel for sinners. Now I discovered that Christ was not asking me to come to Him as a prayed-up, Bible-loving, God-honoring, fully conse-crated, victorious-living, witnessing, successful, soulwin-ning Christian. He was inviting me to come just as a sinner. It was a simple thing, but it was like throwing open the windows of a stuffy room.[2]

After those first absorbing four months, Revel and I were back on the East Coast ready to welcome Joe and William. There-after we moved around as a team of four, sharing the ministry between us, one or another of us coming in with testimony or

---

[1]From *Show me Thy Way,* published by Christian Literature Crusade.
[2]From *Captivated by Christ,* published by Christian Literature Crusade.

an additional insight to complete the message another had given. Our first engagement was a residential conference at Fort Washington on the campus of the WEC, which was sponsoring our tour. People came from all parts, far and near, and every corner of that great old building was filled. They came with a tremendous spirit of expectancy, not only because they had read *The Calvary Road*, but because in Joe and William they knew they were to meet two of the men who had been at the heart of revival in East Africa and who had contributed so much leadership to it.

If in England William Nagenda was concerned about an emphasis or teaching that might take the place of Jesus in the center, he was far more so in America. Here in her strong, lively, evangelical church there was every conceivable emphasis and technique, all of which purported to be the answer to the church's need, but all of which William saw to be competing with Jesus Himself for the central place; and he knew that revival would come from none of these things. As a result, people heard what they never expected to hear. Having read the book, they were expecting talks on brokenness and openness and how they were to be worked out; instead they heard Jesus preached, and after that, Jesus, and after that, Jesus. Out came the little white circle in the center of William's Bible, and again and again he pointed to it, saying, "It is not this or that in the center, but Jesus."

Every conceivable sacred cow was shown to be just that. WEC had its own specialist emphasis on faith, which, it was asserted, was the secret of the life of C. T. Studd, Rees Howells, and its own mission. William and Joe would have none of it—God's plan was that Jesus should be the center, that "in all things He might have the preeminence," as it says in the Epistle to the Colossians—how often they gravitated toward that Epistle on this tour! In his concern William asked that a large card should be placed behind the preaching desk for all to see, with the one word JESUS on it, and I believe it remains there to this day.

John Whittle had designed an attractive brochure for the tour which each church was to distribute, on the front of which was the theme, "Living on Revival Level." Even this William challenged in his zeal for the Lord Jesus.

"Why have you put revival on the front?" he asked the hapless John, who was quite at a loss to understand. "Why have you not put Jesus on the front or something that shows that He is all we need?"

Revel and I, who had already learned these lessons, were quietly saying amen to all that William and Joe were saying, but at times we held our breath.

Of course, it was not long before one of the things enumerated as not to be in the center was *The Calvary Road,* and this puzzled some. Because so many had been blessed through it, they had come to regard it as the handbook of revival. More than that, it represented for CLC their first great publishing success, over which they were even then "sweating blood" in the print shop. But William in holy zeal had cast even that to the ground as a potential idol.

Understandably, some soon came up to me and asked, "Don't you rather resent it when William mentions *The Calvary Road* in this way?"

"No, I don't," I was able to answer. "I stand with him. If that book in any degree is put in the center, it could become a formula that would minister death rather than life. Only Jesus ministers life for sinners."

Now, this was a crucial issue. If I had stiffened my neck and resented what William had said, and if I had tried to defend the book, it would have been the end of it; it would no longer have continued on a course of blessing but rather remained merely a book of the past on a few peoples' shelves. But because I was willing to be broken (a favorite *Calvary Road* expression!) with regard to it and to recognize its limitations, God has gone on and on using it, all over the world.

So the tour continued up to Boston, over into the Midwest, and back to New York. The fact that we were black and white together was a witness to the fact that at the cross all questions of color are irrelevant and forgotten. It was not only that we whites were unconscious of William's color, but he was unconscious of it himself. When in other circles barriers are caused because of color, it is not only because of fancied superiority in the whites but also self-consciousness in the blacks; the latter find it difficult to forget their color. Grace had long since set

William free from that, so much so that in one church, when a white lady rose to give a testimony and said, "I thank God for what He has taught me through our black brother on the platform," he found himself looking around to see who the brother was and had quite forgotten that he was black.

This freedom with regard to color seems to be typical of those East Africans who have been touched by revival. They walk as sons of the King among fellow sons and for that reason are always acceptable in white churches, such men as Bishop Festo Kivengere and the Rev. John Wilson, who have since the days of William often visited America and helped so many.

I pick out just one more incident from that tour because it goes back to a point of prime importance. In one large city we got hold of a Saturday newspaper and turned to the church page—or I should say, pages, for to our surprise the church announcements covered several large pages. For English readers I would say that the church pages in an American newspaper are a sight to be believed! There we saw a spectacular spread of advertisements, many in large type, announcing a healing service in one church, a miracle service in another, revival services in yet another, a noted evangelist elsewhere, special soloists and choirs in yet other churches, and all over the place startling sermon subjects. Joe and William, fresh from Africa, had never seen anything like it, and they shook their heads and sighed, "But where is Jesus?"

That night in the meeting Joe Church in his quiet, almost naive, way said, "I turned tonight to the church pages of the paper and, like Paul at Athens, I saw 'the city wholly given up to idolatry.'" I looked at the faces of the congregation and I thought I discerned their surprise at hearing the multitudinous activities of their churches described as so much idolatry, and I chuckled. But it is true. I myself have sometimes looked at the latest "how-to" book on some aspect of the Christian life with its instructions, methods, and techniques, and I too have said to myself, "But where is Jesus?"

In that tour Jesus was "evidently set forth crucified among us" right in the center—no blessing but Him and by coming to Him. He was seen as both revival itself and the way to revival. As men saw Him, conviction of sin, repentance, and liberation came to their hearts.

What lay behind the ministry of Joe and William at this particular time? It was quite clearly corrective, as it had been in England, though gloriously positive. It was not merely a doctrinal emphasis which they saw in Scripture and which they sought to apply to a situation before them. It was rather a fixed point of reference in their experience, to which they returned again and again either consciously or unconsciously. What they had seen, they had seen and they could not deny it. They had been in the midst of a movement of revival in East Africa ever since 1930 in which the river of grace had flowed "unmuddied" by law and formulas.

Every deviation from the simplicity that is in Christ had been challenged by wise leadership. There had indeed been such deviations from time to time, but from them all the Lord had brought them back again to grace and Jesus Himself. As a result, salvation and holiness had continued to come to numberless lives. Yes, holiness, for revival for them was not merely an increasing number of people being born again, but rather the quality of life manifested in a fellowship of people walking with Jesus, all the time repenting and rejoicing. They could only compare what they met in other situations with this fixed point of reference, and challenge what they saw to be deviations from grace to any form of "striving"—a word often used by them, meaning, trying to get by effort what is already in Jesus.

It might be said that the Holy Spirit does not always work in the same way. That was readily conceded; indeed, any attempt to copy East Africa would have been spotted as another form of striving. Yet, when all our big planning is done, and we have used all our new methods, techniques, and gimmicks, everything is reduced ultimately to what Joe and William insisted on, Jesus and our relationship to Him.

When I returned to England, I found myself talking to a good friend, who, though he spoke kindly to me, was nonetheless voicing the old criticisms that had gone around England about my ministry. Behind his expressions of concern for me I could hear what I knew many others were saying: "What a pity, he used to be such a great evangelist, and now he has gone off on some strange, unbalanced message." Being the man I am, my first reaction was to defend myself and rebut all charges. But when I was alone with the Lord, He said to me, "Why did you defend yourself? Are not some of the things people say the very ones I have shown you, only at a deeper level than they could ever see?"

It was true, of course, and it suddenly came to me that I owed England my testimony with regard to these further things. I accordingly shared all this in the next number of the News and Prayer Letter we sent out, which, while it went mainly to those we were in close fellowship with, did reach some who were not in sympathy. It was really a case of "agreeing with thine adversaries quickly" in what God had shown me, only I was able to say far more about myself than they had ever said. Though this fell into the hands of only a few such people, it was enough to cause some of my old friends to change their attitude toward me. From then on began the process of doggedly living it all down, It is difficult for people to criticize a man who criticizes himself and does so far more than they.

Perhaps the greatest result of sharing this with the wider circle was the effect it had on me. As long as my attitude was "I am right and they are wrong, they'll have to see it one day," I was all the time wondering what they were thinking of me, and I simply withdrew. But once I recognized that I had a testimony to give with regard to these things, I was free. I could go into any circle and meet anybody. I could tell them far more about myself and where I had seen myself to be wrong than they had said about me; and I could do so as a forgiven man. Not that I put myself under a legal obligation to go around telling everyone; I didn't, but I had a testimony to give if and when it seemed appropriate to do so—which, strangely, was not often. My new boldness stemmed from the fact that the blood of Jesus was now my righteousness in these matters. As somebody has said, "The man who is justified by faith need not worry what other people think of him," which means he is free to love them. This was a liberation indeed.

Sixteen

"We Would See Jesus"

IT WAS OBVIOUS to us that we should write a sequel to *The Calvary Road* in order to share the new insights God had given us. We owed it to that large circle of readers across the world who had been so searched and humbled by the first book. We were thankful that it had affected so many, but had they seen Jesus and as a result been lifted up and set free? Had they experienced what it meant to be no more under the law but under grace, or had some of them only deduced a new formula from the book and were they laboring under it, depressed that they could not make it work in their lives? Had they seen the meaning of the blood and had they as a result of that sight ceased from their works to enter into His rest?

All these aspects were there in the first book, but implied rather than fully expounded. It was basically an essay on brokenness, designed to convict the saint and show him where he needed to get right with God. But the Christian cannot live on brokenness and repentance, as we ourselves had discovered. He must learn to live on Christ and to stand on the ground of grace alone—not in the old unrealistic way, where everything was regarded so objectively that there was little subjective experience, but in reality and truth.

So it was Revel and I began to write *We Would See Jesus*. As the time spent on it was snatched from the short periods between meetings and tours, it took a long time. Sometimes

Revel would deliberately stay at home to write. Furthermore, it was not always easy writing a book together. Sometimes when I would come home and read through what she had so painstakingly written, I would go silent, for there were things I did not feel quite satisfied with and I hated to say it. There were tears, as precious pages were laid aside. Perhaps that is why God used it ultimately so much—it had been watered with tears. In any case, some of the most helpful parts were certainly hers.

I wonder if it ever would have appeared, had not the Lord overruled an apparent mistake. We had completed half the book and took it with us when we visited America again for a long tour in 1958. A number of chapters needed revision, and additional chapters needed to be added. But I sent the half which was ready to Ken Adams of the American branch of CLC, that he might express an opinion. I did not want to toil on with the rest of the book, if what we had already written was not acceptable. I heard nothing for several months; so I wrote again, saying I was still waiting for his opinion. He replied, "We have waited eight years for this book, and now you are putting pressure on us as soon as you submit the manuscript. Be patient for a little longer, my brother."

I did not understand that letter, as all I was asking for was an opinion—at least not until a few weeks later, when I received the galley proofs with the whole thing set up in print and a brochure announcing the date of publication. He had gone ahead thinking that that was the whole book! As I looked at it, however, I discovered that the book was complete as it was, one common thread binding it all together and giving it unity. The other half of the book was clearly not needed; in any case I had now little option but to let it go through largely as it was. But I hardly dared tell Revel—the chapters that would have to be dropped were almost all hers!

So it was that, eight years after *The Calvary Road*, there appeared both in America and England its successor, *We Would See Jesus*. Although the first book has had, and continues to have, the wider circulation, the second one follows well on its heels and for me is by far the more important, representing more nearly what I now love to minister. The message of grace is more fully expounded in it, and struggling people more readily find the answer and the way to apply it continually. *We Would See Jesus* does not contradict one thing in *The Calvary Road;* it rather builds on it and gives the fuller picture of Jesus as all we need.

The relationship between the two books is best described in the preface to *We Would See Jesus.*

> In *The Calvary Road* we see now that we were dealing with the effects. In *We Would See Jesus* we feel that God has led us back much more to the Cause. In the first book we dealt with aspects of Christian experience such as brokenness, fullness, fellowship, repentance, submission, holiness and so on; and it is good to be challenged by the effects which God is out to produce in us, although too great an emphasis on the effects may lead to a wrong striving. In this book we are contemplating the wonderful Cause of these effects, the Lord Jesus Himself. Here we do not need to itemize the Christian life; it is enough to see Jesus. He is both the Blessing we all seek and the easily accessible Way to that Blessing. If we concentrate on trying to make a certain aspect of things "work," it will become a formula for us and will lead us only into bondage. But the Lord Jesus has come to take from us every yoke of bondage and to set us free to serve Him in the freshness and spontaneity of the Spirit, and all that by the simple sight of Him which the Holy Spirit delights to give to the needy, despairing heart. *We Would See Jesus* therefore does not go on from *The Calvary Road* so much as it goes back; back from the effects to the adorable first Cause of all.

To put it another way, the emphasis in *The Calvary Road* is on repentance with the grace of God implied. But in *We Would See Jesus* the emphasis is on grace with repentance implied.

I came across the other day the story of how a group of Christians in another land had been greatly affected by *The Calvary Road* as translated into their language. As a result the leader suggested that they all be absolutely honest with one another, hiding nothing. As they opened up to one another, they discovered that all they had to share was their own weaknesses, and this made them depressed. But had they seen the grace of God more clearly, they would have understood that those very weaknesses only made them candidates for that grace and qualified them the more for Jesus, the sinner's Friend. They would have seen the blood of Jesus cleansing them from all which their consciences condemned them for and bringing them into the Holy of Holies by its power. Songs of praises would have filled their lips, and it would have been real revival.

In his book *Life Together*, Dietrich Bonhoeffer makes a trenchant comment on what too often passes as Christian fellowship and in doing so gives by contrast a picture of what true fellowship is.

> It may be that Christians, notwithstanding corporate worship, common prayer and all their fellowship in service, may still be left to their loneliness. The final break through to fellowship does not occur, because though they have fellowship with one another as believers and as devout people, they do not have fellowship as the undevout, as sinners. The pious fellowship permits no one to be a sinner, so everyone must conceal his sin from himself and from the fellowship.

But how do we achieve such open fellowship with one another? Do we do it by sitting around trying to be honest and keep to the rules of a formula? Little wonder that we are struck dumb or depressed. Such fellowship is possible only in the context of the grace of God and as each sees

> Grace is flowing like a river,
> Millions there have been supplied,
> Still it flows as fresh as ever
> From the Saviour's wounded side.

Only as the shadow of the cross falls on a group of people can each afford to be a sinner. Then what is said and shared is far more a joyous testimony as to Jesus giving the conscience peace than a painfully expressed confession of secret things. Seeing the cross where "mercy there is great and grace is free" is the biggest incentive to honesty there is; and what fellowship and love is then experienced!

The fact that *The Calvary Road* has had by far the greater readership only serves to show that that is where the casual Christian must begin. He needs a great dose of conviction with regard to sin and self in his personal life and relationships with others. And if he has an honest heart, he will come back for more and love it. But sooner or later he will have to see grace.

Other books have followed. In 1967 there appeared a slim paperback *Be Filled Now*. Those three words were more than a catchy title: they summarized the heart of the message of grace as it applied to the filling of the Holy Spirit. It is not "be filled tomorrow," when we hope we shall have improved, but "be filled *now*" in the midst of our failure and current need—as we are, where we are. And after this now, the next now. Such an experience of present-day blessedness for needy people is only possible as we are given a new sight of the grace of God making every blessing available on street level.

Be Filled Now was published after lying for years in a file in an uncompleted state; but apparently God had a vested interest in it, as shown by the way in which He gave it a special introduction right across America. A copy arrived on the desk of the circulation manager of the well-known Christian periodical, *Christianity Today*. He took it home, read it, warmed to it, and decided that this was the sort of book that they were looking for to send as a gift to each new subscriber. He accordingly asked CLC to do for them a special imprint edition of 15,000. I was later shown a stack of letters from their readers in which people told of how God had used it and asking for further copies. By that simple means God sent it to corners which it would otherwise have taken years to reach.

Then eight years later in 1975 came *When I Saw Him . . .*, based on the text, "When I saw Him, I fell at His feet as dead" (Rev. 1:17), with the subtitle "Where Revival Begins."

A year later came *Our Nearest Kinsman*, with the subtitle "The Message of Redemption and Revival in the Book of Ruth." I know of no Scripture that presents a better picture of what grace does for the failed saint than the Book of Ruth, nor one that gives a more affecting presentation of the Lord Jesus as our Nearest Kinsman. In the moment of greatest failure He is still our heavenly Boaz, ready to redeem for us all that we have lost.

In 1976 there came out after many delays in both writing and publishing a specialist book, *Forgotten Factors*, with the subtitle "An Aid to Deeper Repentance of the Forgotten Factors of Sexual Misbehaviour." It contains the same old message of the grace of God, but applied to the situations of confusion and misery caused by sexual misconduct. As the friend who was typing the manuscript finished it, she said, "If that doesn't give sinners a hope, I don't know what will!" Amen, sister! My hope is that it will not only be of help to those with problems along this line, but to those who find themselves having to counsel others with them.

Then in 1977 came *From Shadow to Substance*. This is a rediscovery of the inner message of the Epistle to the Hebrews, centered on the words, "Let us go on." All the other books are smaller works; this is a larger one in which I have attempted more. It is, however, not intended to be a merely academic study of the great epistle, but is meant for the hungry-hearted; I trust it will be found loaded with encouraging applications for the neediest reader. My wife says that so much of what she has heard me preach seems to have found a place in that book! It would seem that I have found the epistle strangely flexible and accommodating! Not so really; if the message of grace of God and the blood of Christ is not the message of that Epistle, and indeed of the whole Bible, then I don't want it. But I have found it to be the red cord that runs through the entire Bible. Indeed, the one who follows that red cord will find that he has the key to the whole of Scripture.

Some may wonder why I have been at pains to list these later books. It is because each one represents my own developing vision of Jesus and growing understanding of the message that brings revival and therefore is an integral part of my own pilgrimage. I dare to say that within those pages there is dynamite, for the apparently gentle message of grace which they contain is the power of God for the accomplishment of moral and spiritual miracles.

I pause at this point to look over what I have set down and I fear that the record may give the impression that all my activities have been devoted exclusively to things spiritual, such as preaching and writing. This is far from the case. When we seek first the kingdom of God and His righteousness, He gives us to enjoy the earthly side of life too.

It is true in my early days the Lord convicted me of certain hobbies which had become idolatrous and usurped His place in my life. It is also true that when I surrendered these to Him, I had no other aim but to serve Him, and virtually no other interests obtruded. But years later as I grew in the Lord, He began to give me liberty to enjoy other interests and hobbies also. I think they were needed to preserve balance.

For instance, I became an avid photographer and was one of the first to develop the idea of synchronized soundslides, i.e., color transparencies with tape narration and on-the-spot recordings. At conferences abroad I presented quite a sight, draped with cameras, lenses, and microphone, making a photographic and audio record of it all. Sometimes I had qualms as to whether all this was diverting me in some degree from the intense spiritual battle we were engaged in. However, when the record was completed and shown at home, it proved such a spiritual blessing, not only to our summer conferences, but to other groups too, that I was comforted.

But it is a fine line that we all have to draw between what is fitting and what is inordinate. We must each one be open to the Holy Spirit to show us. Dr. Joe Church helped me on this point once. He has been a hobbyist himself, though supremely a missionary doctor and revival leader; he and his sons loved to build their own boats on the lake near his mission station in Rwanda. He said that what often determines the rightness of our special interests and enthusiasms is whether we can bring others into them or whether they can be used for their benefit and enjoyment.

That helped me with regard to my photography, but I had difficulty when I got involved in stereo. My involvement began with the gift of an old outsized loudspeaker. I hitched it to my tape recorder, but that was not powerful enough to get the best out of it; so I bought myself a good stereo amplifier. That was the beginning of the slippery slope! If I had a stereo amplifier, why not a turntable with a stereo pickup? And if I had all that, why just two odd loudspeakers which did not match one another, why not . . .? And so on and on it went from one thing to a better thing. However, having enthusiastically acquired this equipment, I was disappointed to find that Revel was not the least bit interested. Indeed, she looked upon the whole thing as a nuisance, and it troubled me: had I been right? That night I could not sleep, and when she had fallen asleep, I rose and went to another room to seek the Lord. I turned to *Daily Light*, the little book that contains a selection of Scripture texts for each morning and evening. There I saw two verses, taken from different parts of the Bible but put together in perfect juxtaposition. "My God shall supply all your need according to His riches in glory in Christ Jesus." That was encouraging; but the next verse challenged me: "Let your conduct be without covetousness, and be content with such things as ye have." I was immediately convicted that I had not been content with what I had, that there had been a covetous spirit in my heart. I confessed this to the Lord, put the whole equipment, so to speak, under the blood of Jesus, and found peace with God. Strangely, this did not mean my having to get rid of it; rather He gave it all back to me with liberty to enjoy it. Since then I have progressively assembled a library of some of the world's finest music which others have enjoyed with me.

The Christian life, then, is not only concerned with high and holy things, but with such earthly minutiae as these.

Seventeen

Marital Oneness

I COME NOW to share a painful experience, which, although grace has long since healed it, I would prefer to draw a curtain over. It was the one occasion when our marital oneness was seriously threatened.

Now, any couple willing to walk in the light with God will find Him often revealing day-to-day attitudes and words that hurt the other and for which they will need to ask forgiveness. As I understand it, if a couple are seen to be deeply one with each other, it is not merely because of natural compatability, nor because they seem to have attained some high spiritual plateau, but because they are often repenting at the feet of Jesus together, where His blood cleanses from all sin. Only by this means are barriers removed as soon as they come. This had been the way Revel and I walked ever since the Lord met us in revival.

But this incident was more serious and painful than the day-to-day experiences of repentance. I share this story only because it illustrates important spiritual principles, which some may be able to apply to themselves and thus receive help. So, for your sake, dear reader, I share what otherwise I would prefer to keep private.

I must go back to one of our visits to the United States. In one place we found ourselves ministering to a group who had recently been experiencing the gifts of the Spirit, such as speaking in tongues—it was the early days of the charismatic movement. We were praying with them, and at one point Revel felt they were waiting for her to pray in this way or to ask God that she might. Whether that was really the case, I do not know—I was unaware of it; there had been nothing unusual in the other prayers. The effect on her, however, was to cause her afterward to ask the Lord whether the gift of tongues was for her.

The Lord seemed to say to her, "What do you really want?"

"What I need and want above all else is love," she prayed, "love for You and love for other people."

"If that is what you want," He replied, "you know the way."

Now, this was not just a pious prayer on her part. She had long known that this was her lack. She had a distinguished appearance, always composed; and I think some people used to find her a little unapproachable. Occasionally someone would confess that they felt fearful of her and ask her forgiveness. Such openness with one another might seem strange, but not among those with whom the Lord had been having deeper dealings and who were "walking in the light, as He is in the light." In that light everything that causes barriers is seen as sin—even fear—and needs to be cleansed in the blood of Jesus.

Although the persons who mentioned this to Revel were concerned only to confess their own sin, it always made her search her own heart. She came to see that if people feared her, it was because she did not love them, she was not as outgoing and caring as she should be. When therefore she said, "I want love," she really meant it. And when the Lord said, "You know the way," He really meant that too. And she did indeed know the way: that of calling sin, sin and coming to the cross of Jesus for cleansing. She had taken that way over many matters, but not clearly and specifically over this. But now she did so; lack of love was seen as sin, and at the feet of Jesus she received what she confessed she lacked. Although she received no dramatic experience, from then on there was a gradual but definite increase of love in her life, and she began a caring ministry for others she did not have before.

This ministry, however, created a problem for me—I began to feel left out. She was having an intimate touch with people that I did not have, and I was not always told of it. On one occasion I found her writing a letter, which instinctively she covered over when I came into the room. When I gently removed her hands, I found it to be one of the most caring and discerning letters that one person could write to another in need. Why she should want to hide it from me will be understood as I continue with the story.

Calls for the revival message had begun to come from a number of other countries, and in my enthusiasm I had strung a number together to form a world tour. First, West Pakistan and India, where Joe Church and I would team together. Then he would return to Uganda while I continued on to Australia and New Zealand, then to Hawaii, thence to the West Coast of America, right across to the East Coast, and then home across the Atlantic, the whole thing to last some five months. Revel would not be going with me, as such a tour might be too much for her health, and in any case she had the responsibility of handling the mass of registrations for our summer Holiday Conference and much else. But she was never happy about my going on this long tour, and she said one day:

"Roy, if you keep arranging these long tours while I stay at home, you will find we will draw apart from one another. I will develop my own circle of fellowship and sphere of activities this end, and when you get back, you will feel out of touch and be jealous." These words proved all too prophetic; but by this time I felt too involved to withdraw.

On the eve of my departure for Pakistan there were several telephone calls to our home which I answered, and each time I called out, "It is for you, Revel." They were to do with her caring ministry, but I seemed to know little or nothing of what it was all about.

High up in the plane, all the way to Karachi, the devil gave me a bad time, and my heart all too readily responded.

"What is this touch Revel has with other people?" I asked myself. "Why has she not told me?"

As I sat there for hours on end, it all loomed larger and larger and I could think of nothing else. And, of course, in my mind it was Revel who was at fault.

By the time I got to Karachi and met Joe, I was in bad shape. He had been having his battles, too, but of a different sort; he had been suffering grave injustice at the hands of another. We spent the whole of the first evening alone together pouring out our troubles and hurt feelings, and I do not think we were much help to one another. What I needed was a clear, straight challenge as to my attitude, which was wrong. But can you believe it, the Lord blessed that tour mightily nonetheless. I would just manage to crawl to the cross before each meeting and confess the turmoil in my heart, and immediately the power of the Holy Spirit would be felt in the meetings. In one large gathering of Pakistani ministers, almost half of them were on their knees at the end praying for mercy, some admitting they had never been born again. But after every such meeting, back would come the old thoughts, resentments, and battles.

I do not think I have ever suffered so much as I did in those two months in India. I tried desperately hard to get things right with Revel, writing to her almost daily and waiting anxiously for her replies; but although they went by air they seemed to take an age, and when they did arrive, they came out of their due order. On two occasions I even made telephone calls from India to London, but all to no avail. We only succeeded in making one another more unhappy.

I can see it all so clearly now—I was plain jealous, and what I needed to do was to repent and confess just that. I did actually recognize the jealousy, and even tried to repent of it, but I kept on insisting that Revel was wrong too. That is no repentance at all which at the same time points at the other. That was the simple source of all my trouble—blaming the other and not being content to get peace with God as the only sinner in the situation. There is absolutely no solution to our troubles while we are still pointing at another.

In our exchange of letters I learned why she had not shared with me her various concerns for others—why, for instance, she had wanted to hide that letter. She felt that I could not enter into them and would despise her for taking the trouble. But what sort of man did that make me out to be? Quite obviously a man so without love as to be unable to understand. I was prepared to admit that; but if it was so, why did she not help me with it, as she had helped others? And so the battle raged in my mind.

I realized that I could not go on with the tour. As I had so often taught, what is the use of preaching to others when things are not right between a man and his wife? I therefore wrote letters asking those in other countries who had made preparations for my coming to release a brother in grave need. I left Joe to complete the rest of the schedule in India, while I flew back to London.

Revel met me at the air terminal, and without waiting to get home we went immediately to a nearby hotel lounge and talked and talked. I had still not reached peace when Revel made me listen to what God had shown her. One of her friends to whom she had confided everything had simply said, "What Roy needs is to be loved more."

She realized that although she had asked God for a fuller love for other people—and He had given it—she had not maintained the appropriate differential with regard to her husband. She had had an increase of caring for others, but not a similar increase for me. She was so sorry; would I forgive her? As so often happens, the woman beats the man to the cross. Revel certainly got there first in this case, but I had so much more to be forgiven. And so at the cross two sinners were reconciled to one another. The blood of Jesus cleansed away all the guilt and shame and we became more one than ever, with a mighty increase of love on both sides.

Shortly after I returned home, I went to a conference where I met many of my friends. I felt I had returned as a failure (which, of course, I was) and that they all would regard me as such. After all, I had freely circulated among them my impressive itinerary and asked their prayers for it. What would they say when I turned up halfway through?

One of the first to greet me was William Nagenda. He said, "Praise the Lord, Roy, that you were weak enough to return halfway through!" What a thing to say! But he said it because he saw clearly, as did so many of our African revival brethren, that acknowledged weakness is the way to victory. I hugged him for it.

Eighteen

The Lord Gave and the Lord Hath Taken Away

IN 1967 I had the traumatic experience of losing Revel, and I had to say with Job, "The Lord gave, and the Lord hath taken away."

The facts of Revel's homecall are briefly these. It took place on our way home from the month-long Holiday Conference at Clevedon, Somerset. Great numbers had passed through the conference in the four weeks, and many had met the Lord in a new way. The expanding team had gathered from all over the country. On the spiritual side it had been an outstanding time of blessing. We had both shouldered big tasks, Revel undertaking the catering, and I doing the general organizing and giving spiritual leadership. Revel herself had been specially used by God. In each of the four weeks she had delivered a message which had proved to be the turning point of each week, coming virtually from the kitchen to give it. It was a gift God had given her to bring just the right message for the right moment. This had been so recognized by the team that she only had to say, perhaps hesitantly, that she thought God had given her a message, and the team would stand back to let her speak.

Everything was over, and all the guests had gone home. After a few days' rest we were on our way home ourselves, the car packed with equipment, a real sense of "mission accomplished" in our hearts. We were driving on the Portway, a big road on the outskirts of Bristol, when suddenly the next thing I knew I was in an ambulance, knowing there had been an accident, but having no memory of it at all. I learned afterward that a truck on the other side of the divided highway had skidded across the divider and into my lane. We collided, and a four-ton container was wrenched off the truck and fell onto our car, squashing it right down to the ground. Mercifully I remember nothing of this at all.

In the past, noting how the Lord calls His own home, I had made the observation that He always seemed to do so with the utmost courtesy. Perhaps that is what is meant by the verse, "Precious in the sight of the Lord is the death of His saints." Though the sudden and tragic way in which Revel lost her life might not seem to have much courtesy about it, the blow for me was softened in so many ways that it proved to be the kindness and mercy of the Lord indeed.

On that dramatic night it was as if we were passed from one of His sentries to another all along the way. Never once were we out of the care of His people. The car immediately following ours had Christians in it who saw it all. The lady who held me in her arms as I lay unconscious by the road was one of the Lord's. The man on ambulance control that night was a Christian who had been on holiday in Clevedon and had come night after night to the tent and had been blessed through the meetings. When he heard the call come over the air, "Smash on the Portway, send ambulances," he said to himself for some reason, "I wonder if that is Roy Hession on his way home."

"We have got them," the message crackled on the radio a little later. "The name is Hession, but we have not got their Christian names, nor their address yet."

"I know their Christian names," he answered, "and I know their address." He found himself the only one, he thought, who knew who we were, and began to phone around in an attempt to inform Christian friends.

When I got to the hospital, I asked, "Where have you brought me?"

They said, "To the Bristol Royal Infirmary." I knew it well, for we had lived in that city in the fifties and had many Christian friends there.

The doctor in the Casualty Department said to me, 'I think I know your name."

"Are you a Christian?" I asked.

"Yes."

"Do you know Melville Capper?" I asked. "Get Melville for me, if you can." He was one of my dearest friends in that city, a leading surgeon. It so happened, by chance almost, he was on the premises at that very time and was at my side in a few minutes.

"Melville, find out what has happened to Revel," I said. He came back to tell me that Revel had been called home, and he wept over me as we prayed together. She had been killed instantaneously and had gone to be with the Lord without a moment's suffering. I could only give her back to God who had first given her to me.

Meanwhile, Mrs. Capper had made some telephone calls and set God's bush-telegraph in action. That night, my doctor son, Michael, and my close friend, Ken Moynagh, one-time missionary doctor in Rwanda, arrived in my hospital room from other parts of the country.

The courtesy of the Lord in what seemed to be an otherwise tragic thing was especially seen when Michael and Ken Moynagh gently told me, as doctors, that for a long time they had had grave fears for Revel. As previously recounted, sixteen years before she had nearly lost her life due to a pregnancy that had gone wrong. Ever since, she had been living with a dangerous blood pressure, and had been able to do so only because her heart had compensated for the extra load.

"But," they said, "it could not have gone on; sooner or later she would have had a stroke and been paralyzed. Her work would have stopped and yours, too, as you would have had to give up your traveling to care for her. God has taken her that you might continue the work He has given you."

I saw the kindness of the Lord. Her mission was accomplished, and she was called home instantaneously, while I was spared because, apparently, the Lord had further work for me. All was in the loving, almighty hands of Jesus, and He had done what He had with infinite courtesy.

During those days I was given an amazing experience of the love of the brethren. The very next morning John Collinson entered the room, having come from his home in another part of the country, and from then onward the door of my room was hardly ever closed, as brethren and sisters came from all over the country to express their love and sympathy. It was then that I began to weep, not for my loss so much, but because I was melted with this extraordinary love of God manifested through the brethren. Those two weeks in the hospital were the most intense time of Christian fellowship I have ever known.

What touched me and helped me was to realize that this was a corporate loss. Revel had been a means of blessing to so many, and had become so close to them in caring fellowship, that in many cases their sense of loss was almost as great as mine. "She belonged to us all in a deep way," wrote one. I found myself weeping for them, as I imagine how stunned and bereft they must be.

God used her homecall in a remarkable way, however. One of the team wrote, "Suddenly there has been made real the fellowship that has been slowly forming over the years as, with you, we praise for her whose life now appears like a pure, clear, shining light. The purpose of her homecall is already becoming evident. We are learning to love one another as a fellowship as never before. We have been melted together over the telephone and in numberless church porches and homes. Many of us are feeling that we want to give to Jesus every bit of life we have left. I cannot explain how it has affected me—it is as though everything has shifted and the center of gravity has come right. If this is what happens to everyone else, the result will be tremendous."

The funeral took place at Alma Road Chapel, Bristol, the Brethren Assembly founded by George Mueller, which I used to attend when living in Bristol. I was able to be present at the funeral in a wheelchair. Those who had but recently returned home from Clevedon now came back from all over the country, several hundreds of them; two had traveled from Scotland. Ken Moynagh, Stanley Voke, and John Collinson gave messages full of sweetness and the triumph of the Lord Jesus. Someone afterward described it as Revel's valedictory service. It was one of the most moving and triumphant times that many had experienced. One of the speakers wrote to me afterward: "I wish you could have been on the platform and seen the expression on people's faces. It was like the sun bursting through the clouds on a rainy day. In the last hymn, 'With harps and with vials there stands a great throng,' some appeared as if they had looked into heaven. Dear Revel, like Samson, God has used her in her death more than at any other time. For I really believe her death is intended to be the means of a turning point in our fellowship, as though what we have been feeling after and longing for in all these years, what we have had glimpses of at other times, has suddenly burst into full flower—a real fellowship of brothers and sisters who really love one another."

Perhaps the culminating moment was when around the graveside we heard Lawrence Barham speak the words of the promised resurrection in the Lord Jesus, and I asked them all to sing:

> Glory, glory, hallelujah,
>   Glory, glory to the Lamb;
> Oh, the cleansing blood has reached me,
>   Glory, glory to the Lamb.

Revel and I had spent twenty-nine wonderful years together, years in which we learned how to walk with Jesus and how to repent; years in which we made new discoveries of the grace of God, and how our very spiritual poverty and need only qualified us for that grace. They were years in which we were privileged to take that message all over Britain and the United States. For eighteen years she was the real inspirer and architect of the summer Holiday Conferences, toiling ceaselessly on the catering side and yet sharing from the platform in the spiritual ministry. She used to tell me that she had almost a physical sensation when God was giving her a message. At these conferences hardly ever is a team member asked to deliver one of the evening messages; it is up to him to say if God has put a message on his heart for us, so that the team may decide before the Lord. It was not easy for a woman to do this even occasionally when so many ministers were on the team, but God gave her grace.

She never wanted to be old. Indeed, she knew she never could be in her condition. She once told a friend that she would like to be taken just as she was talking to somebody. And that is how the Lord took her. The last thing I can remember saying to her on that fateful day was to put something right with her. While on the complex of roads entering Bristol, I had been unwilling to take her advice and as a consequence took a wrong turn; but I had justified myself. She said nothing, and I was inclined to drop the matter—with myself in the right, of course. But the Spirit whispered I was not to leave the matter there.

"I'm sorry," I said. "I was quite wrong over that question of the way."

"Thank you, darling," she said, and so we drove on in peace until the crash.

I would like to include here just two testimonies that came in with regard to her, both of them, strangely, from the United States.

Mike Markham, a Baptist pastor in California, wrote:

> How I recall in Oakland in about 1953 when I first heard Revel speaking and the message came like new life to my heart. I was attending seminary at the time, but my heart was far from filled with the Lord Jesus. The sweetness of her voice, the love and devotion I felt was in her heart, the message of repentance and grace, it filled my expectations that at last I had found the way. I recall how the Rev. Paul Peterson and I left that day for dinner and talked. He said, "Mike, no more bulldozing in my ministry; I will change and love my people to Christ." Then at Turlock some years later, she spoke after you, Roy, on the subject, "Outside the camp," where the Lord Jesus died for us. It melted my hard heart that day. I found release and the waters began to flow. You asked me to give the benediction that morning and I was all ready to shout— the Master had come. It was a change in my whole life and ministry when I began to walk with Jesus in the way of repentance and faith. For years I had been striving to climb the rungs of the ladder of self-attainment in prayer and devotion. But I found that He had already come down—down to my sinfulness and blessed me.

Betty McJunkin wrote from Seattle: "You and Revel were the ones God used to begin His deep work of repentance five years ago in the hearts of my husband and me. I remember wanting to sit by Revel so that I could watch her. The peace and rest she had were so apparent in her life, and I could not keep my eyes off her. She had something I didn't have, nor had I seen it in any other Christian I had known. She was a gracious, queenly person and yet when I talked with her, I felt she was like my sister and on my level. Her honesty in sharing and opening her heart so freely impressed me much, and the Holy Spirit used her to begin to reveal the deep need I had, though I had been so blind and thought I had no need."

My son, Michael, and his wife were full of caring for me. He was the first to be at my bedside in the hospital, having disrupted his holiday to do so. In a masterly way he undertook all the arrangements for the funeral; and when I was fit to be moved, they lovingly received me into their home while my fractures healed. And they did everything possible to encourage me to take up the threads of my life again.

Nineteen

The Lord Took and the Lord Hath Given Again

THE LORD IN His mercy did not allow me to struggle on alone for long, for He brought Pam Greaves into my life and in 1968 we were married. I was able then to put Job's words the other way around: the Lord who took has given again, blessed be the name of the Lord! It was not merely because of His mercy to me that He did this, but because He had a vested interest in the ministry He had entrusted to me, and He knew I needed a partner if I was to fulfill it.

Pam had herself spent various periods totaling nine years in East Africa as a secretary in the Church Missionary Society and was identified with the revival brethren there. During one of her longer spells at home, lasting five years, she occupied the apartment above ours in southeast London. She became very close to Revel, especially when I went away for meetings on my own. She had gone through the throes that many a single girl on the mission field does, and by the way of repentance had come through to a testimony that Jesus satisfies—even without a husband. Pam had previously been met by the Lord when that first team from East Africa visited her church in Surbiton in 1947, and she has her own story to tell of her pilgrimage from law to grace since then.

Usually a second marriage meets most resistance from the family. In my own case they gave me the strongest encouragement, for one day Michael asked, "Have you ever thought of marrying again?"

163

"No," I said, "but in any case, who?"

"Pam Greaves," he replied.

He told me that he and his wife had always appreciated what they had known of her.

With that in mind I looked again at Pam. The first time I permitted myself really to do so, love sprang up in my heart and the Lord seemed to whisper in my ear, "She is My choice for you," although, of course, I said nothing to her then.

That God should be guiding in this direction so soon after Revel had died was a problem indeed and one in which I needed the fellowship of my brethren. But I could hardly share it with them as a whole when the principle character in the drama was blissfully unaware of the part she might have to play in it. Therefore I decided to share it all with just Dr. Ken Moynagh and his wife, Wendy, as representative of all my brethren. I may say there were many long telephone calls to them from my bed in Michael's home, where I was still recuperating. They had known Pam in Africa and were quite overwhelmed at the love of the Lord, if this was the provision He had made for His tried servant. Thereafter each step forward was steeped in prayer together. We felt it was right that I should make a first innocuous approach to her, and it proved to be, strangely enough, on the matter of clothes. I telephoned her at the office of the Ruanda Mission where she was working and said, "I need to buy myself a new suit, and I am hopeless at colors [which was perfectly true!]. Could you possibly come with me and help me choose something?" I thought the confession of male helplessness was one way at least to a woman's heart!

"And be sure," Wendy Moynagh had said, "to bring her home to us for tea afterward."

It was not long before we were able to speak about our mutual feelings and know the Lord intended us for one another. This was no mere marriage of convenience, so that I might be able to continue my ministry. A love was given us as deep and fresh as that which had characterized my first marriage.

We were not lacking signs of God's guidance. Godly friends seemed to have a personal revelation—or should I call it a premonition?—that this was what God was going to do and were not the least surprised when they heard. In one case it was much more than a premonition. I was having a meal with some old friends and said hesitantly that I was thinking of marrying again, and one of them said, "I know; I have been told."

"Who told you?" I asked.

"I had a dream the other night," she replied, "and I saw Revel in the inexpressible joy of heaven. And when I asked, 'But what about Roy?' I was told, 'He will marry Pam Greaves.'"

This was all the more remarkable, because our intentions had been kept a closely guarded secret and, in any case, these friends had barely met her. Other unusual confirmations were added, so much so that the whole matter seemed to be heavy with destiny.

We certainly needed such confirmations, for we were soon to find our course being contested. We had been brought together far earlier than was conventional—we were married just six months after Revel had died. We therefore felt that the fact that we knew well in advance what God was planning ought to be kept secret, out of deference to other people's susceptibilities. Gradually we leaked it to those we felt closest to on the team. Whereas most rejoiced with us and encouraged us, especially those who had known Pam in Africa, others were shocked and distressed. It was not, of course, that they disagreed with my marrying again or had any objection to Pam, but the timing disturbed them. It was said that if I married again too soon and did not allow something like a year to elapse, I would ruin my testimony. How could the guests at the next summer Holiday Conference bear to see me with another wife, when they had so loved and appreciated Revel? I think I suffered more as a result of this opposition from some of my brethren than at Revel's passing.

Yet I was comforted again and again by a succession of encouragements from the Lord to indicate that He did not expect us to wait for the conventional period of a year.

First, something Ken Moynagh said displayed his deep understanding of the nature of things.

"The period of a year," he said, "is simply a convention the world has established because of sin. If there is a second marriage earlier than that, they will suspect there was something wrong going on before the passing of the first wife. But among the saints, where all is in the light with God, there is freedom."

That helped me to see I need not be bound by what Paul calls "the elements of the world" (Gal. 4:3).

On another occasion, when I had received a hard letter on this subject, I heard a quotation from Bishop J. C. Ryle, the great evangelical leader of a former generation, who had been bereaved and remarried three times. He said that if he lost his present wife, he would immediately ask God for another, so highly did he esteem the boon of a godly wife. I could have hugged him, had he been around!

On yet another occasion we went together to visit friends to whom we have been close over the years, the Rev. Peter Marrow and his wife, Barbara. Peter and I had often joined forces in revival ministry and Pam knew them well, as she had been part of the fellowship that met years before in his vicarage at Surbiton. That day Barbara said something significant.

"At first I was shocked when I heard that you were planning to marry again so soon. And then I realized that marriage is only for earth and to help us on earth. In heaven 'they neither marry nor are given in marriage, but are as the angels of God.' Perhaps in our fellowship we have made too much of Christian marriage, thinking it was for heaven too."

Then one day, standing outside church, feeling somewhat depressed, we met a couple who were of mature years, both of them Christians, who told us happily they were engaged to be married. The man had lost his first wife on the precise date I had lost Revel. And when I asked him, "And when do you intend to be married?" he mentioned the exact date which we had in mind for our wedding. It was just another whisper of encouragement from the Lord.

Then Satan began to contest our proposed marriage in another way. Pam became what I would call "calamity-conscious" and had fears that something terrible would happen to prevent our ever getting married. "After all, one calamity has already happened," said Satan, "how do you know another is not on the way?" She began to develop certain physical symptoms that suggested something was seriously wrong with her, and we wept together before the Lord. It is good for a couple sometimes to weep together.

I said, "I don't know what this means medically, but to me it has the smell of sulfur about it" [i.e., it was from Satan]. "It is not like the Lord to put a delectable cup to our lips, only to snatch it away when we are about to drink."

The Lord gave us Jeremiah 29:11 in one of the more modern versions: "I know the plans I have for you, plans of welfare and not of calamity, to give you a future and a hope." This was just the encouragement we needed, and it came from heaven. We dried our tears and began to walk by faith again. How quick we had been to believe the worst and entertain gloomy thoughts of God, thus maligning His love!

With a heart that was nonetheless sinking a little, I took Pam for a thorough check-up. There was nothing major wrong, and the Christian surgeon simply said, "Forget it!" Forget it we did, and all those symptoms disappeared—and with them the smell of sulfur!

A final, almost unbelievable, confirmation came that same evening after the surgeon's verdict. We went to have dinner with the couple I have mentioned who were planning to marry on the same day as ourselves. My first words on meeting them were, "We've just had a reprieve," and I told them the verdict of the surgeon.

"I've had a similar reprieve too," he said. Then he told us how as soon as he began to move in the direction of marrying again, he began to have pains in his chest in much the same way as his wife had had. He was quite sure he had lung cancer and would never live to marry again. He went to a top consultant, who found nothing wrong and who said to him much the same, "Forget it!" His symptoms, too, all disappeared. As we listened open-mouthed, it was as if the Lord said, "This is My final confirmation for you. No need for you to have any second thoughts and ask yourself, Did the surgeon miss anything? Your clearance has come from Me."

And so it was on March 2, 1968, six months after Revel had gone to be with the Lord, that Pam and I were united in Holy Matrimony from the home of her brother, the ceremony taking place in a tiny eleventh-century church near Saffron Walden,

Essex, surrounded by a few of our relatives and our closest
brothers and sisters in Christ. Lawrence Barham, by that time
a bishop, conducted the service, speaking on "As for God, His
way is perfect." Ken Moynagh, who had stood with us and
encouraged us in the troubled times of our engagement, was
our best man; our beloved William Nagenda, now a very sick
man, was there with his wife, Sala. And as we walked down the
little aisle to the door, husband and wife, our dear friend, Fred
Barff, played the organ—not Mendelssohn's Wedding March,
but the revival praise chorus,

> Glory, glory, hallelujah,
> Glory, glory to the Lamb!

Every one of those saintly men I have just mentioned has since
been called home, as also has Sala Nagenda, far earlier than we
ever expected. "Part of the host has crossed the flood, and part
is crossing now."

With regard to our joint life and ministry since then, it has
seemed that Pam has simply taken over, after a short hiatus,
where Revel laid her work down—rather like two runners in a
relay race, where one passes on the baton to the other in the
same team. Pam and I have traveled Britain and other countries together, passed on God's Word together, and for some
years shared the onerous tasks of the annual summer Holiday
Conference.

I have never ceased to be amazed, not only at the oneness in
our personal relationship which the Lord has given, but at the
identity in our understanding of the truths of God. Although
our personalities rightly and properly differ, we seem to think
as one person when it comes to the deepest things. As we travel
the world, she will sometimes add a word to my message that
exactly enforces its emphasis, just as Revel used to do. There
seems to have been hardly any break in my pilgrimage and
ministry.

Twenty

Into Other Lands

FROM THE MOMENT some of us were blessed through the message of revival, calls started to come for this message to be preached in other lands. We in Britain were one of those "other lands" to which that first team came from East Africa, and as we became established in the vision, calls began in turn to come to us. As I was free for itinerant ministry and did not have the responsibility of a church, I was able to respond to these calls. In any case, the wide dissemination of *The Calvary Road* in other countries made it easier for me to be introduced there.

It was not long before we discovered we did not need to depend on any book. The message of grace, of which Jesus Himself was the center, was self-authenticating. Whether or not people had read this or that book, they had only to be exposed to the message in one short series of meetings and they thirsted for more, and calls to other churches and to other countries would come. Thus I spent an increasing amount of time in other lands. Indeed, some years my wife and I were more out of Britain than in it. Over that period I visited no less than fourteen countries in Europe, North and South America, Asia, and Africa, some places again and again. These have been no sight-seeing tourist trips, but stern and demanding assignments; yet they have been joyous experiences too, as the service of the Lord invariably is.

These tours meant, of course, speaking by interpretation.

The message seemed to lose nothing in the process, not even when the English had to be translated into two languages as, for instance, into French and German. Where the interpreters were people of ability (and they usually were), every shade of meaning was transmitted and understood, as could be seen by the varying expressions of the congregation. Usually our interpreters were spiritually one with us and would get completely lost in the message. The radiance on their faces would give added meaning to the words they were uttering. Indeed, they were not merely translating the message, but making it their own and preaching it every bit as much as I was. Certain interpreters—Ernst Krebs in Switzerland, for instance—have stood by my side for innumerable hours, and a tremendous bond of love has sprung up between us. They seemed to know what I was going to say even before I said it, and I am sure they went on to preach those messages themselves long after I left; nothing pleases me more than when I hear that is so. Strange as it may seem, the occasions over the years when I have seen the Holy Spirit working most powerfully have been when I have been speaking by interpretation.

These tours abroad were undertaken usually in team with another brother or with Revel in the earlier years and Pam in the later years. We in England had learned something of team work in revival ministry from our brethren in East Africa. The first brethren from there came to us as a team of four missionaries; then we had seen William Nagenda and Yosiya Kinuka taking meetings together, as also Joe Church and William; and when some of us visited East Africa, we found that this was assumed to be the natural way. And we had put it into practice in Britain in our various activities, notably in the summer Holiday Conferences. In the mouth of two or three witnesses every word is established, and sometimes the message becomes, as a result, quite irresistible. More than that, it gives the ministry a much wider spectrum and greater depth.

Such teamwork could be costly, at least to self. We found that sometimes the subtle desire to be appreciated more than the other crept in and with it jealousy and criticism; and we had to be willing to go to the Lord together for Him to make us one again. But in this way the very thing we were preaching was happening in the team, which became a living demonstration of the message, for we often liked to testify as to how the Lord was helping us together.

The vision that has always been before me on these tours has not been of merely scattering seed wherever we went. That, of course, is a good thing and it is always wonderful when individuals get a new and transforming experience of the Lord. Our vision was that ultimately those newly blessed individuals would become so related to one another that they became a team with a vision for their country, or at least for their particular area. In other words, it was that a bridgehead of revival should be established, no matter how small, in which Calvary love for one another should be experienced, and through which the Lord would move out further. This, of course, is something that only the Holy Spirit can accomplish, and it takes time, sometimes a long time. But in various countries and in varying degrees it has happened.

I can only speak of what I have seen. Other brothers have seen as much, and more. The travels of my friend Bishop Festo Kivengere, himself a product of revival in East Africa, are far more wide-ranging than anything I have been called to, and he could tell much more than I of the spread of revival blessing across the world.

Nothing would be served by a mere recital of these tours of mine. I only mention those visits abroad where I recall something which is relevant to the story of my personal pilgrimage, or more important, has something to challenge us today.

FRANCE

My first experience of revival ministry abroad came in 1949. William and Joe were back in Europe, and they suggested that Peter Marrow and I should join them on the team to answer a call which had come from Guebwiller, France. The secretary of the Scripture Union in France at the time, Léonard Bréchet, had been met by the Lord through the East Africa team three years before, just as we had. Guebwiller, his headquarters, possessed extensive camp grounds. He had planned to make the last week of his summer season a revival conference with the four of us as the speakers.

This was my first experience of speaking by interpretation, in this case into French and German—indeed it was my first journey by air. Revival had given me wings in more ways than one! Intense interest had been aroused, and the camp was packed with people from France, Germany, and Switzerland, with many from the immediate district.

I have three special memories of that time.

First, there came a moment when we sensed that the break—or rather, the melting—had come, although we were not giving any open invitations. At the end of one meeting a man got up and asked if he could give his testimony. Joe looked at his watch and said—it seemed to me, rather casually, "No, not just now, I don't think we have the time."

I became upset over this and said, "But, Joe, you are grieving the Spirit just when He is beginning to work."

"You need not worry about testimonies, Roy," he replied. "The time for the people to give their testimonies is when they will burst if they don't!"

So it proved. A day or two later an opportunity was given when they were indeed at bursting point with newly experienced joy in the Lord. We sat and sat, as people poured out their testimonies about God's dealing with them, while we had the English translation whispered in our ears. That meeting lasted two hours. Even so, they were still not through, and we had to set aside another meeting which also lasted two hours. That is how it is when the Spirit really sets men free. I learned from that not to push.

A second memory relates to one particular testimony in that meeting. A man rose to announce himself a Prussian, who had fought in the First World War and who under the Kaiser had learned to say, *"Gott Straf England"* ("God punish England"). He told us that when that war ended, all his hate had died away. Then he had fought under Hitler and again he had said, and meant it, *"Gott straf England."* But that war ended, too, and once again his hatred vanished.

"But," he said, "when those Englishmen appeared on the platform, and when I saw that one of them [and he pointed straight at me] looked exactly like Winston Churchill [not the first person to say that!], all my bitter hatred returned. But," he added brokenly, "I have repented and I ask you to forgive me!"

Thereupon he marched up to the platform, threw his arms around Peter Marrow and myself, and gave us a kiss on both cheeks with his bristly moustache, while the congregation broke out into a song of praise to God! I learned later that this was not a case merely of a believer getting readjusted with the Lord, but that for the first time that day he was born of the Spirit and became a true Christian.

The third memory is of an incident that took place after the conference was over, an incident which has a special meaning for those who pray for revival. Everyone was leaving amid much rejoicing and many embraces, when one group who were returning to a nearby town came up to us.

"We've been praying three times a week for three years for revival," they said, "and, of course, we shall continue to do so now more than ever. Tomorrow is our next prayer meeting, and we ask if you would come and speak at it."

We agreed without giving it much thought. But the next day just as we were about to go into the meeting, the whole situation dawned on William. He took hold of Joe's arm and said, "Stop a moment! Do you realize that they have been praying for revival for three years and now they propose to go on doing so? They just haven't seen the Way yet."

What he meant was this. Jesus had come to us all in a new way; as a result, the captives had been made free, the spiritually blind made to see, and the morally lame to walk again. If that was not revival, what was? They still had a mental picture of what they expected. They had not seen that Jesus Himself was the end of the struggle for revival. They were still praying as if revival in Him had not come.

William went into the room to give an astonishing message, "right off the cuff." He told them of how in the Gospels all the people were expecting the coming of the Messiah. They were all waiting for Him, some doubtless praying earnestly, when all the time He had already come. One stood among them whom they knew not. What they needed to do was to recognize Him who had come and acclaim Him. William then applied this to their prayers for revival, as if it had not come, instead of recognizing Jesus as all the revival they would ever need, and falling at His feet; what a message! It was really but another illustration of the same truth expressed in the story of the woman at the well. She had said, "I know that when the Messiah cometh, He will tell us all things."

"I that speak unto thee am He," Jesus replied.

So often the saints talk and pray earnestly about revival and say, "When revival comes, this and that will happen." Jesus answers, "I that speak unto thee am revival—get right with Me now and you have revival."

The conference at Guebwiller became an annual one for some years and was deeply blessed by God. I went again and again to share in it, and Léonard Bréchet and I became close friends.

SWITZERLAND

It was while Léonard and I were driving along the German autobahn one day in 1957 that the Lord gave us the thought of an international revival conference. If it was to be international, where else could it be held but in Switzerland? Accordingly the Grand Hotel, in Leysin, high up in the mountains above Lake Geneva, was booked for a week in June 1958 and was filled with some four hundred of us. People gathered from other countries in Europe as did some from East Africa; there were even two ministers from California.

The brethren responsible on the Continent decided that, although they could not expect it to be an international conference every year, they would make it their own annual one. So it has continued for twenty-one years, and for more than half of those occasions I have been over to participate with the team there. Others of our brethren from England have traveled over too, and a deep link has been forged between the two teams.

Three other annual conferences have sprung from Leysin, designed to serve different age groups and language areas. This shows how a bridgehead established in a few hearts will slowly expand until a significant movement of new life runs through the churches.

As an alternative to the picture of the expanding bridgehead, we can use that of the Gulf Stream, that warm current that flows from the Gulf of Mexico right across the cold waters of the Atlantic, bathing the shores of England and Northern Europe and giving those countries a more moderate climate. Revival is something like that. It is not necessarily something spectacular, not even obviously different from what is already happening, no more than the Gulf Stream looks different from the

Atlantic. But it *feels* different, and the spiritual climate along its course is always warmer. Revival is the Gulf Stream of the love of the brethren that flows from Calvary through the all-too-cold waters of our churches. Thank God for all those countries where the Gulf Stream is flowing—like Switzerland.

GERMANY

Germany has proved exceptionally receptive to the message of grace. I cannot remember how the first call came for me to go there, but I could spend almost another life going through Germany, following the trail of the Spirit.

I have had the warmest relationship with Brockhaus Verlag, the well-known evangelical publishing house, and they have translated several of my books into German and sent them on their course of blessing among the Christians.

Germany fell in love with William, so much so that the influential Pastors Prayer Fellowship got him to give them no less than six months. These theologically minded men were content to sit at the feet of this simple African with his message from heaven and learn from him.

Bishop Festo Kivengere is another from East Africa who has been visiting Germany in more recent years, sometimes in association with Billy Graham. He has such a positive, compelling message, overflowing with grace and truth, that the Lord has given him great favor with the German Christians, especially with the young people.

BRAZIL

Brazil is the largest and most important of all the South American countries. It is so rich in natural resources that it could one day rival the United States in wealth, if it could only beat the scourge of corruption. Only the influence of the gospel of Jesus Christ can accomplish that, and it is bidding fair to do it. The gospel is winning more converts and at a faster pace than perhaps anywhere else in the world, and that in a country which is nominally Roman Catholic. It is said that the Protestant churches are doubling themselves in membership every ten years, and that by conversions alone. New churches are being started all the time, at first in storefront rooms, but soon developing into full-grown churches with their own complete premises. But there are dangers in this situation of enthusiasm and growth, chiefly that of "striving"—i.e., the substitution of human effort for the working of the Holy Spirit and the stressing of different emphases which prove divisive.

The call came from Don Phillips, an American missionary in Brazil who had introduced Youth for Christ there. We met in Los Angeles in about 1958, when he was on furlough, and he immediately knew that the message I was seeking to give was what Brazil needed. He urged me to go there for a tour, with him handling arrangements. I confess I felt flattered, and was inclined to go on my own. Whereas we are indeed sometimes called to go on commissions on our own, and whereas there is nothing binding about always teaming with another, the Lord on this occasion showed me that I was wanting to dispense with my brethren, and He said, "If you think you can do without them, you think you can do without Me!"

That finished me. I immediately asked Joe Church if we could respond to this call together. How glad I was that I did, for it proved to be one of the most strategic assignments we had known, and it needed all the wisdom each could contribute.

I give no details of that particular tour except one significant story of a man whose life was transformed at that time.

Joe and I were leading a ministers' conference in some campgrounds near São Paulo when Ernie Gilmore, a young American missionary with the Presbyterian Mission, flew in from his station in the mission aircraft. A great hunger of heart had brought him. In conversation he told us of the barrenness on his station and the defeat in his own life. The missionaries had grown so cold that if one of them talked seriously about the Lord, the others would jokingly say, "He's talking like a missionary." He told us how recently Don Phillips had given him a copy of *The Calvary Road*, and the Lord had begun to work in his heart again, showing him things which he must put right, in some cases with his colleagues. He told us how, as a result, a new fellowship had grown up between the missionaries and there was a new blessing on the work. We suggested he might give his testimony in the meeting that day. He did so. As he concluded the story of the Lord bringing him back to the cross in repentance, he said, "However, I cannot say I am filled with the Spirit yet, but I am seeking."

Afterward I drew him aside and said, "While I praise God for your testimony, I was disappointed to hear you say you are not filled with the Spirit." As we talked further, he began to see that he did not need to go any further than the cross to be filled with the Spirit. There Jesus was made to him all he needed. And as he had come to the cross, God had indeed filled him with the Spirit, because of the power of the blood—if his faith would receive it. There he began to believe in the value of the blood of Jesus for him. On subsequent days he could be seen in quiet corners, under the trees, and elsewhere, bowed in wonder and worship, believing it all—cleansed in the blood, therefore filled with the Spirit, and Jesus all he needed, his righteousness with God and His holiness within. He returned to his station radiant, emancipated.

As he humbly gave his testimony there, the Lord used it to make others hungry. Christians began to repent, and others began to seek Christ for the first time. He wrote back, "Roy, it's rivers of living water!" How simple and well within our reach is God's way of being filled with the Spirit.

As a result of what happened to Ernie, some of his fellow missionaries came to later gatherings and were likewise helped. This resulted in their mission in Brazil officially sending a call for a return visit. So it was the very next year, 1960, I went back, this time with William Nagenda.

The Lord made William and me deeply one and we came to "love one another with a pure heart fervently." Our messages seemed like the two blades of a pair of scissors. The obvious oneness between a white man and an African was very affecting to the Brazilians, and they had no defense against our message. We were served by interpreters—the young Artur Gonçalves, the evangelist Walter Kaschel, the banker Danilo Vasconcellos, and a godly sister Clemen Moreira. They wore themselves out as they stood beside us in the heat, hour after hour, but they entered joyously into what we were saying, and in differing measures it became their own experience. Each of them, and many others too, were to become very dear to Pam and me on later visits. But these were early days, and we had no idea in which hearts God was going to establish His ongoing work.

During a gap of twelve years none of the overseas brethren visited them. When we remembered how much we in England owed in the early days to the constant visits of brethren from East Africa, we realized we had neglected them in Brazil. However, when ultimately Pam and I went in 1972, it was to find that those brethren who had been touched twelve and thirteen years before were still walking in the good of what they had learned. As for the people at large, they had never forgotten the impressions they had then received. The news went around, "Those people are here again; you know, the ones with that message that so touched our hearts twelve years ago." And they flocked to the meetings and followed us around from church to church in São Paulo.

Three years later we went yet again for just three weeks and then only to the city of São Paulo. It was one of the most action-packed three weeks of my life—the Spirit's action, not ours. At last we realized that God had established. His bridgehead, the fulfillment of all the hopes behind our previous visits from 1959 onward. But it had taken sixteen years to happen; God was not in a hurry. That revival foothold today is getting even deeper and stronger, the circle is expanding, and from it have come precious leaders with the authentic revival vision.

I give something of the story of Artur Goncalves, that young man who translated for us on the very first visit and whom I always have loved since then, because there are points in it with which many can identify.

Shortly after that first visit, he had entered the Baptist ministry but, unknown to me, had gone through all sorts of vicissitudes in the intervening years. When Pam and I went to Brazil in 1972 after that long gap, I was looking forward to seeing him and anticipating with pleasure having him interpret for me again. However, he did not show up for a week or two, until finally he came to a minister's conference. I greeted him warmly and said, "You're going to translate for me, aren't you?" He was very diffident and not at all sure that he would. All the sparkle had gone out of him. Well, he did translate for me, but he was not at ease. Then he told me what had happened.

In the intervening years Artur had had domestic trouble, strains between him and his wife which were quite widely known among his minister friends. The Lord had helped him and it had been resolved, but the shame was still there. He did not feel he could stand up on the platform beside me and interpret, since the ministers all knew. This sense of shame had taken away his boldness, and he felt there was a black mark against him. As we discussed this together, he saw and appropriated the power of the blood of Jesus, not only to forgive the initial wrongs but especially to cleanse the consequent shame, his inhibitions with people (what are they thinking of me? etc.). He saw he now had a testimony to give, not so much about the original matter, but much more with regard to the resulting bondage, from which Jesus had now freed him.

In coming months Artur let his testimony be known, and his brother ministers loved him. They began to feel, strangely, that he had something they had not, and they invited him to take the lead in different areas of his denomination. When Pam and I returned three years later, he arranged the whole program for us. There he was interpreting with joy by my side the very message that had set him free, and they all knew that it had. Jesus not only forgives the sin, but transfigures the situation and gives us back more than we have lost.

INDIA AND PAKISTAN

The story of India and the blessing spreading from East Africa is one that only the Holy Spirit could have thought up. In 1951 Bishop Appasamy of the Church of South India became concerned about the whole question of revival and called a conference. There various leaders were to read papers on past and present movements, each having had a revival allotted to him for study. Cyril Thomson, who had gone to India as a missionary with the Bible Churchmen's Missionary Society and had then been transferred to pioneer Youth for Christ there, was asked to make a special study of the revival in East Africa and present his findings. He knew nothing of it, but sent to England to obtain whatever literature there might be on it.

As Cyril studied the scant literature, he found his attitude changing from an interested observer to one who was being deeply and personally involved. In short, he came under conviction of sin and met the Lord Jesus in a deeper way than ever before. He was then able to present not only a paper, but a fresh, personal testimony!

The result was that very soon an invitation was sent to two of the leaders in East Africa, and Joe Church and William Nagenda made a tour of various centers in India to share with hungry Christians what God had been teaching them. It became a spiritual revolution for many, and some leaders were marked for life. Joe and William followed this visit with a second one, and later still another tour was undertaken by two others from East Africa, Festo Olang and Erica Sabiti (both of them later becoming archbishops). The result was that there were numbers of leaders in various parts of India who had a new experience of the way of the cross.

In 1960 Cyril invited me to come with another brother, and on this occasion I went with Yosiya Kinuka. Yosiya was the very first to be brought to Christ in the revival in Rwanda—it is a historic story—and has been one of the spiritual leaders ever since. There had been a special attachment between us ever since he came to Britain in 1947. He is a man of few words from the platform, and his messages are models of brevity, but they go deep and are powerfully used by God. His homespun illustrations are unforgettable and quite inescapable in their meaning. My messages are, I confess, anything but brief. He invariably said, "You go first, Roy, and give one of your Bible Readings [he always used to call my messages Bible Readings!] and I will follow." I would start at length and take all the time I needed, and Yosiya would conclude with a short word. He was quite happy with this arrangement, but some people came to ask, "Why is it that Roy preaches so long whereas Yosiya speaks only briefly?"—doubtless thinking that I had not left enough time for Yosiya. So I insisted that on the next few occasions at least, he should speak first and I would follow. When speaking first, however, he was just as brief, so we laughed about it.

On one occasion Yosiya and I boarded a plane at an Indian airport after a long wait, during which we had paced the tarmac while talking together. On the plane a curious Indian gentleman asked us who we were and what we were doing. When we told him, he replied, "I thought as much. When I saw you two walking up and down together, engrossed in conversation, I said, what in the world can these two have in common, a white man and an African? I told the friend with me that I thought you must be missionaries or something similar."

We were happy to tell him that what we had in common was

Jesus. Fellowship in Him that transcends color is always a powerful witness to the world. Our questioner proved, by the way, to be the treasurer of the Church of South India.

Yet another incident from that tour demonstrates the reality of the Spirit's work in our midst. In Pakistan I was in full flight in my message with Bishop Chandu Ray, the Bishop of Karachi, translating, when he stopped me. He immediately gave a word of personal testimony to the people in their language, relevant to what I had been saying, and then we continued. There was certainly the ring of reality about it.

INDONESIA

In 1963 the call came to Willian Nagenda and me to visit Indonesia. This was before God gave the great revival in that land in 1967, which has been so widely reported among Christians through the world. The call came from Detmar Scheunemann, a young missionary with the Worldwide Evangelization Crusade, whom we had come to know and love when we first met him in Germany. Together with Pak Octavianus, one of Indonesia's leading evangelists, he had played an important part in the leadership of the Bible school at Batu, Java, which later became the watershed of the revival in 1967. Detmar has always said that what the Lord did in 1967 grew out of what He did for them during our visit in 1963.

Indonesia is a mighty country, said to contain the fifth largest population in the world; and yet its land mass consists simply of a string of islands, over a thousand of them, stretching from Asia to Australia. They are mostly volcanic in origin, and on a number of them the volcanoes are still active. It is not an uncommon thing to see wisps of smoke issuing from distant mountains. On a later visit a group of us climbed one of these volcanoes and looked down into its rumbling inferno. Just as I was about to change the lens on my camera, it slipped out of my hand and we watched helplessly as it rolled down into the crater. It did not disappear quite into the cavernous opening itself, but got stuck halfway down inside the slope. To my astonishment, Volkhardt Scheunemann asked our Indonesian guides if one of them would go down and fetch it: not surprisingly, there were no volunteers! Quite apart from the obvious danger, the volcano was sacred to them as the home of one of their gods. So somewhere up there in one of the volcanoes of Indonesia is a lens of mine, or what remains of it!

William and I confined ourselves to the principle island, Java, starting at the capital, Djakarta. We found the heat and humidity almost unbearable. William, though used to Africa, wrestled with it even more than I did.

"The only thing to do," said Detmar, "is to say yes to the climate."

I did not want to say yes to it, but when I did, it was easier.

We traveled the whole of Java's hot, humid length, having fruitful meetings at various places en route. We noted everywhere the lush vegetation—no drought or famine here. We admired the carefully laid out rice fields, terraced right up to the top of every hill, the terraces bequeathed to them by former generations.

When at last we came to Batu, which lies at the eastern end of the island, we instinctively felt that to visit the Bible school was the main purpose of our coming. The conference here was for the students of the nearby secular University of Malang, the Bible school students acting as hosts. About one hundred and fifty grand people turned up and stayed four days on the campus. Some of them had very little knowledge of the gospel, and there were even a number of Moslems among them. William and I had the privilege of giving all the messages. How God blessed us! Seldom has the gospel, the message of good news for bad people, been so living to us. We saw the Lord Jesus, and so did the young people. Many came to know Him for the first time, and others who had got away from Him returned to Him in deep repentance.

Those are the outward events. The inside story is that I experienced a new humbling before the Lord. William's messages had a way of reaching the hearts of the girl students, many of whom were in great need. At the end of one meeting in particular there was a great line of them waiting for him to counsel them. Detmar set aside a room for him and gave him a senior lady to act as interpreter, and he counseled those girls far into the night. But no one was lining up to be counseled by me—just one or two fellows, but certainly no girls! So instead of just hanging around, I went to bed and lay there feeling critical and miserable. I said to myself, "He deliberately preaches to the girls!" I was clearly jealous. It was not that I wanted especially to be counseling girls, but it was that line of people waiting for him and none for me that rankled! At last I had to confess that I was wrong, not William, and the Lord gave me a word with which to come to Him: "He whom Thou lovest is sick," the message that Mary and Martha sent to Jesus when Lazarus lay dying. I confessed to Him that I was sick and could not get out of it, but I was still loved by Him. So a sick man that night rested his head on the breast of Jesus and got peace.

I shared this with William the next morning, and he said, "Roy, there is just no one helping these women and girls, not even the older Christian women, and I must do what I can. It is not easy for me, and I know it is dangerous. Sometimes I get impure thoughts, especially when a girl cries. But I repent and Jesus cleanses me and I go on with the work. I feel rather like a soldier who gets wounded in the battle, but who does not give up because of it. He ties a bandage around the wound and continues with the battle."

In 1972 I went to Indonesia, this time with Pam, and Festo Kivengere joined us—a nice team of three which we enjoyed immensely. Once again the call had come from Detmar Scheunemann at the Batu Bible school. God had indeed poured out His Spirit in the revival five years before. It had begun with His bringing conviction of sin and deliverance to the students. As a result, these newly blessed students went out to the islands of Indonesia with the gospel, and the power of the Holy Spirit upon them. They saw the Lord do mighty works as they testified for Him, so that sometimes whole areas were turned to Christ. In some places a considerable breach for Christ was made in the wall of Islam.

This turning of the people to Christ was often accompanied by unusual manifestations. It became quite commonplace for the Lord to speak to people through dreams, which often resulted in conversions to Christ, and this among people who were otherwise quite out of touch with the gospel. But there had been other manifestations, which really deserved the name of miracles. Indeed, it could be said that there is hardly a miracle in the New Testament which had not been reproduced at one time or another in those years in Indonesia, notably on the island of Timor. Those miracles had never interested me; I had feared that if they received undue emphasis, they would take our eyes from the Lord Jesus—and that would be the end of revival.

That is what actually happened, especially on that island where most miracles were reported. The immature converts there had become too miracle-minded, and when certain miracles did not happen, they forced them, or rather simulated them. This had caused such a scandal among the church leaders—not all of whom were in sympathy with the revival—that they vowed they would never have any more preachers from Batu. We were ourselves due to go to Timor, but our visit had to be canceled for this reason.

The Bible school was also in a time of need, especially the faculty. New missionaries had come out who had not been through the revival fires. They did not understand the level of fellowship which had obtained in those days, and the others had adopted subtle attitudes toward them which were not helpful. This was not clear to us at first, but as Festo and I ministered virtually in our blindness, the Lord in His own way uncovered the root of the problem and healed it.

With regard to the whole matter of revival and miracles, Festo made a superb comment when reporting on this visit in his newsletter afterward:

> After an initial impact of unusual manifestations in the revival, the Lord Himself is becoming the drawing magnet of this people's desire for full salvation. This is as it should be. Such manifestations often do occur during the early stages of God's outpouring of spiritual blessing in times of revival, but they have subsided here, as they usually do. This seems to be a normal trend, as far as one can judge. Some observers, attracted by the spectator and romantic aspects of the miraculous, have over-reported this side of the revival here. Now things are taking the normal spiritual shape, and the center is becoming the Lord Jesus Himself. This is the secret of continuing times of refreshing which come from the glorified Lord Jesus.

We heard a short while later that the trouble on Timor was resolved and, we trust, with miracles in their proper place, so that the people are all set for continuing revival with Jesus Himself in the center, other things taking whatever shape, spectacular or unspectacular, that the Lord may choose.

Lest I be tedious, I pass over without comment visits to Uganda in 1968, South Africa (under the Dorothea Mission) in 1971, whence we went to Dar-es-Salaam in Tanzania for a most unusual mission with Festo Kivengere and others. Here I found myself preaching in the Roman Catholic cathedral night after night, and doing so with the blessing of God upon it. It was crowned with the conversion of the Anglican dean. In one year alone, 1971-72, Pam and I were in three continents. I pass on now to speak of the last continent I would mention here.

NORTH AMERICA

Here in the United States and Canada I have spent more time overseas than in any other country. To date I have made no less than thirteen tours for periods lasting from three weeks to eight months and have moved all over the continent. So extensive have been the periods I have spent here, and so vast and varied the spiritual scenario, that to report on my experiences would require a book in itself. From my first visit in 1952 I have been conscious that these years have been America's day of grace, and I have worshiped God for it. This has become more apparent to me with every subsequent visit. The gospel is preached and loved in America more than in any other country, and a harvest is all the time being reaped for the Lord on a scale unknown elsewhere. If ever a nation, as a nation, can be said to be turning its heart toward the Lord, it is America at this particular time. The readiness of people in all walks of life to accept the Lord Jesus as their Savior in their hour of need is for me a constant source of praise to God.

It is here that there has been the greatest response to the message of grace we brought, and it is here that *The Calvary Road* and my other books have had greatest effect. As a result of these visits I feel I have a large number of brothers and sisters in Christ to whom I feel bound in the ties of love. The land is so big that it is impossible to say that there is one team, one bridgehead; there are blessed bridgeheads and blessed teams in all sorts of places. The Gulf Stream of revival is flowing in different areas, some of which I am sure I am unaware of. And that Gulf Stream needs to flow: in spite of America's day of grace, the waters even in orthodox, Bible-based churches can be very chilly apart from the Lord working deeply in revival. Even in such churches there is all too much "casual Christianity."

Most of the tours I have undertaken in North America have been with Revel and Pam, but sometimes with another brother. There have been two occasions when I went with Stanley Voke, a Baptist minister in Surrey, England, and one of my closest brothers, for tours in 1965 and 1971.

Stanley and I seem to have the same cast of mind and the same way of handling a passage of Scripture. So much is this the case that we find it very difficult not to preach one another's sermons when we are on our own, because what one says appeals so naturally to the other. That is, of course, a great help when, in working as a team, we have to pick up and carry on from one another, for we always expect both to speak in any meeting we take as a team. This has been a good discipline for us, for left to ourselves we normally like to take plenty of time.

How is it possible for two men to work together as a team, when both are preachers? We found that all we had to do was to decide who was to start, that is, who had a clear message on his heart. The other would not be too concerned to prepare anything beforehand, but would just sit and listen to his brother. As he did so, his heart would be pollinated and he would rejoice at what he heard; by the time he had to speak, he would be full of matter with which to complete the picture his brother had given. Sometimes Pam would add some telling word of testimony too. So it was that though there were two speakers, or even on occasions three, there was only one message. I remember Armin Gesswein saying after such a meeting in California, "That gathering was heavy with God's presence."

On one tour in 1965 an intimate matter that occurred between Stanley and myself had more important results than we realized at the time. As we traveled in the beautiful car loaned to us, we shared the common American experience of an accident on the highway—an unpleasant one. We were not seriously hurt, though I wrenched some muscles in my back which were very painful; but we were able to continue with the meetings nonetheless. We had been on the go for weeks and weeks, and in view of the pain in my back, I began to indulge the hope that I might slip off back home to Revel and allow

Stanley to complete the last two weeks on his own (why is it that some men always want to run off to their wives?). I mentioned the matter to Stanley and he was not averse to it.

People kept saying that they were praying that the Lord would heal my back, but deep down I did not want my back to be healed: I wanted to get home. As I was making plans to that end, I had less and less peace in my heart, until at last I stood clearly convicted of wanting to run away and of not being willing to "fall into the ground and die" as to my preferences. Stanley and I were occupying neighboring motel bedrooms, and I went into his room and made my confession.

Stanley, deeply moved and almost in tears, replied, "I too have been wrong; I've been wanting you to go. I've grown tired of teamwork and I was looking forward to completing these days on my own. Forgive me, brother." There we were, equally sinners, I repenting of one thing and he of another, but reunited at the cross of Jesus.

So we went on together, and how glad we were that we did. In those remaining days as we moved up the West Coast and into Canada, God did things which we could never have dreamed of, things that ultimately had repercussions right across Western Canada. We came ultimately to Prairie Bible Institute at Three Hills in the province of Alberta.

P.B.I., as it is commonly called, is one of the outstanding Bible schools of North America; it is certainly the largest, even though it is situated in the middle of the prairies, miles away from anywhere. A vast company of its students over the years have gone out to the mission fields of the world. We were there, not for a special conference, but just for an ordinary Sunday; we were faced nonetheless with a congregation of some twelve hundred—Bible institute students, Christian high school, faculty, staff, and local friends.

That one Sunday morning was to prove a deeply significant time in view of all that came out of it. Both of us spoke, I beginning by contrasting the phrase "Found wanting" (Dan. 5:27) with "found in Christ" (Phil. 3:9). Stanley followed and, speaking extempore, gave a message full of grace and power on the cities of refuge from Numbers 35. I can remember his outline to this day: "He shall run . . . he shall tell . . . he shall stay. . . ." Although we were not at pains to make an open invitation, we both knew God had worked mightily in our midst. There were certainly not wanting those who came up to us afterward to tell of what God had done for them that morning.

One of these was Bill Liner, a worker on the home board of a missionary society which had its headquarters in the little town. He had wept his way back to the cross of Jesus and at the end of the service was radiant. He was to become a close friend and colleague in coming years and one who was to make his own special contribution to revival. But let him tell his story of what happened that day.

February 1965 is a monumental landmark in my life. Like Jacob when broken and conquered, I, too, saw the Lord Jesus. It would never have happened "but God" led Roy Hession and Stanley Voke to reroute their return trip to England to include Three Hills, Alberta, Canada, in their itinerary.

A few weeks before their coming I said to my wife, "I am finished with the Lord's work. I cannot go on. I am a complete failure." These words were not the result of introspection but of three weeks of conviction and revelation of self by the Holy Spirit. Flight reservations had been booked for my return to the States and secular employment. Twenty years of working mostly in the flesh was enough. Like the blind leading the blind, I was at the end. My life was defeated, my service was wearisome, and my heart was empty. In utter frustration and despair, I had decided to leave the ministry after twenty years of Christian service.

Such an embarrassing decision was a smashing blow to my pride; as a pastor and one who held a leadership position in a foreign mission society, I had achieved a measure of success—that is, until God began to answer the prayers of some of us for revival. I never dreamed God would answer in this way! My own inner personal failure and hard, unbroken attitude toward co-workers in our mission were being dealt with by God. For three weeks I had hardly been able to eat or sleep. I had no desire to attend any meeting or see anyone. At times I thought I might be becoming mental.

When I heard that Roy Hession was to be one of the speakers at the Prairie Bible Institute Tabernacle, I did not want to go. I literally cringed inside. Twelve years previously I had met him on one of his first visits to America at Fort Washington, Pennsylvania. In that conference the Lord had done a deep work in my heart and I had given a testimony to it. But now, twelve years later, at the end of myself, Roy was the last person I wanted to see. I was afraid he would scold me for my spiritual state. However, God overruled! As I sat in the first meeting and listened, it was as though Roy and Stanley knew all about my life; but as they spoke, a ray of hope began to shine through. They shared of themselves quite personally, which in a very real sense was the key that helped me see the way for a sinner to come back to God. I literally wept my way to the feet of Jesus while they spoke.

At the close of those services, I went to Roy and made myself known. Rather than rebuke me for those years of wilderness wandering, in the most gracious manner he said, "I know exactly what you have gone through. I've been right there." As one sinner to another, he encouraged me in Jesus. What a burden was lifted! A new day began in my life. How and where it would lead was in His hands, but for me, I could lift up my head because of His precious blood. He told us to stay right where we were and prove His faithfulness. Doing this meant going to many individuals and several churches and repenting of pride and hypocrisy, of a hard, unloving spirit, telling them I wanted Jesus to be seen rather than the old Bill and asking them to praise with me that "whereas I was blind, now I see."

Later Bill and Les Simons, one of the students who had also met the Lord that day, became very close, and at the call of the Lord they went out as a team of two to the churches to give their testimony and share the message of grace which had changed their lives. As they did so, God brought revival to the saints, and the blessing in one church provoked calls to other churches, and so on. Wherever they went, there was left a trail of revival and a new song of rejoicing, among the pastors in particular. Their path took them right across Western Canada.

Bill Liner then began to invite those who had been blessed and were hungry for more to come together for a summer Camp-Out Conference in the Rocky Mountains. So greatly was everyone helped on that occasion that it was decided it should be repeated and the same the next year, until now it is an annual event to which increasing numbers are drawn. Indeed, we now look upon it as the Canadian counterpart to our own summer Holiday Conference in Britain and we sometimes exchange speakers.

How glad Stanley and I are that we were both willing to be broken together at the cross of Jesus that day in California!

Right up to the time of writing, further calls continue to come from these and other countries, and various itineraries are still being planned—all of them following up the trail blazed by the little book, *The Calvary Road.* Furthermore, Pam and I are still criss-crossing Britain, which remains our chief sphere of ministry. It is only as we learn more deeply the lessons of brokenness and revival, along with our brethren in our home country, that we have the right to share those lessons further abroad.

Obviously this man's pilgrimage is not yet finished. With Paul in Philippians 3, I want to forget those things that are behind and reach forth to those things that are before, ever seeking to apprehend more fully that for which I have been apprehended of Christ Jesus. That for me does not mean passing on to new supposed truths or emphases, with the danger of getting off course, but going deeper at His cross, where I have already begun—deeper brokenness, deeper appropriation of Christ Himself.

In saying this, I have in mind the old story of a small company in the early days of gold mining in South Africa. They sank shaft after shaft, finding gold in each, but not enough to satisfy them; and so they tried yet another. Ultimately they discovered that all they needed to have done was to have gone deeper in the first shaft; and as they did so, they found gold in abundance. I testify that although I have tried all sorts of different shafts, hoping for greater results in my life, Christ has now become the end of all my searching. Revival for me has meant coming back to the place where I first began, and I intend to stay there. Tell me not now of any other way. But I need to go deeper at His cross—much deeper.

Twenty-One

A Last Look Back

As I LOOK AROUND me today I find myself with doors open all over the world for the ministry of the gospel of grace and of revival, and with more to do in God's service than I have strength for. Then I look back and remember that time in 1951 when every door in England was closed against me. And the irony of it—or should I say the wonder of it—is that the very message that closed those doors in England has opened these other ones all over the world. This does not prove me to have been blameless, but only God to have been gracious and to have owned a penitent man as His own. I thank Him for it.

What about England? I believe we can say we have lived down virtually all the opposition and criticism. We have swamped it with grace. I and my brothers have all the doors to God's people open to us that we could desire. I believe we have the ear of the Christians of Britain as never before. In a day of different doctrines and emphases, we have returned to that place where we began, the cross of our Lord Jesus Christ. I believe we can say with our brother, Ken Moynagh,

> When different winds of doctrine blow,
> Then set their sails who will,
> But as for me, content I go
> To Calvary's lonely hill.

And I trust that as the dust settles, people will know where to find us.

The summer Holiday Conference that came into being as the direct result of revival coming to some of our hearts has continued over a period of twenty-seven years. Thousands all over the country have been renewed in their spiritual lives. In 1974 John Collinson took over from me the heavy burden of its administration, even giving up his parish to do so, though I myself am deeply involved with him in the team which undertakes the spiritual ministry. Under his winsome leadership it has taken a leap forward both in spiritual power and in numbers. Nearly two thousand persons, including children, pass through it every year. Yes, the Gulf Stream is certainly flowing in Britain.

As I look back, I would say just two things as regards myself.

First, I have been loved—loved not only by the Lord, but by my brethren. When Pam heard of the death of Idi Krebs, wife of Ernst, our very dear interpreter in Switzerland, she just said numbly, "She loved me." As I think of many another to whom I have been close and who have been called home before me—William Nagenda, Ken Moynagh, Fred Barff, Léonard Bréchet, Lawrence Barham, Emmanuel Baumann—I can say of each one, "He loved me." And not only those who have been called home, but various ones still with us around the world. I have been embarrassed by their love, their concern, their constant prayers for me. I don't know why they should do it. I cannot say I have always loved. I am not naturally a lovable man. And yet perhaps I do know why: their love for Jesus has spilled over to me—because somehow I have been identified in their minds with the One they love and I have tried to point to Him. I have no complaints with regard to my brethren. I have been loved.

Second, I have been forgiven. Like the children of Israel, how often have I provoked the Lord in the wilderness. Everything they did there, I have done, and yet Moses could say, "Thou hast forgiven this people from Egypt until now." I can say the same.

Forgiven from Egypt until now. On that plank and that alone I will one day escape the wreckage and make the shore.